SILENT DISCO
BY LACHLAN PHILPOTT

CURRENCY PRESS
SYDNEY

australian
theatre for
young people

G T C
R H O
I E M
F A P
F T A
I R N
N E Y

CURRENCY PLAYS

First published in 2011
by Currency Press Pty Ltd,
PO Box 2287, Strawberry Hills, NSW, 2012, Australia
enquiries@currency.com.au
www.currency.com.au
in association with
Griffin Theatre Company, Sydney.

NATIONAL LIBRARY OF AUSTRALIA CIP DATA

Author:	Philpott, Lachlan 1972–.
Title:	Silent disco / Lachlan Philpott.
ISBN:	9780868199016 (pbk.)
Dewey Number:	A822.4

Contents

Typeset by Dean Nottle for Currency Press.
Printed by Hyde Park Press, Richmond, SA.
Front cover shows Sophie Hensser and Meyne Wyatt.
Cover photograph by Michael Corridore.
Cover design by Interbrand.

For Penny

INTRODUCTION

The first draft I read of Lachlan Philpott's *Silent Disco* was back in October 2008. At that time I was working as Producer, Young Audiences at Sydney Opera House. On first reading, the characters and the suburban landscape leapt from the page with immediacy and authenticity, and although at that time the House was not in a position to commission a subsequent draft, Lachlan and I spent the next year in dialogue—working together on the play at Playwriting Australia's National Playwriting Workshop and quickly putting together a rehearsed reading with actors for an audience of school students at Sydney Girls' High School. The young audience gave the play a resounding thumbs-up and afterwards we engaged in a lively discussion interrogating the moral compass of the play's protagonists. Over time the text changed—Lachlan is never one to do massive rewrites after hearing the play read once or even multiple times over one week. Hearing the play read with the right voices is always crucial—never more so than here, with such demanding, rapid narration.

From the beginning Lachlan's writing style was prominent. As Alyson Campbell observes in the introduction to *Bison* and *Colder*, Lachlan doesn't rely on dialogue as the main element of his dramaturgy but more interestingly adopts 'a range of linguistic devices to create a world that is both external and internal to its characters... particularly, a "scene-setting" narrative voice that often does not belong to a character, or voice their internal thoughts, but creates the atmosphere around characters'. Although this latter device is shared between characters in *Silent Disco,* it is the central voice of schoolgirl Tamara Brewster that frequently comments on, and in turn brings alive, the classroom atmosphere, as in this wonderful response to teacher Helen Petchall's question on the importance of having an opinion and being able to express it:

Yawn/...
Mexican yawn/...
Mexican yawn flying round the shit box. (p.7)

The classroom environment of Lachlan's *Silent Disco* is a world of boredom. Disengaged students look for any kind of distraction rather than engage in the here and now. It is a world peopled with long-suffering teachers who are constantly waiting; waiting for the attention of the classroom, for students to answer their questions, for the drone of the aeroplane flying overhead to pass, or for the bell signalling the end of another period. There is tedium and pointlessness to the events that occur within the walls of the classroom on a day-to-day basis; student after student passes through these four walls and, like Helen Petchall, we question what becomes of them.

Lachlan manages to capture this world directly and authentically—as an ex-teacher himself he has been there and knows the terrain only too well. He knows implicitly what Petchall faces each day—in particular, the never-ending battle to attract attention over an iPod. It is a confrontation with a generation that tunes out and retreats into its own pulsating soundtrack with a tiny piece of technology that allows them to remove themselves from the immediacy of their own experience. Confiscation becomes a tug of war, as the dreaded iPod is tucked under collars and hidden in hair, providing relief from the discussion of S.E. Hinton's *The Outsiders*, unbelievably the same text that was taught in my high school in the 1970s.

The microcosm of the classroom and interaction between students and their teachers is a world where nothing ever changes, but everything changes. Lachlan's analysis and reflection on this intensely structured world highlights its incredible impact over the shaping of all of our lives. Through Petchall's frame, we consider the position of the teacher in this world. We wonder at the endless stream of students who have passed through the doors and disappeared without notice, leaving behind assignments uncollected and ambitions never realised. Through her we learn of the strange behavioural codes around students coming to the staffroom, career expo travesties, teacher conferences on how to keep challenging students in the classroom and staff meetings where bitter and angry teachers want to punish students by cancelling the school formal, potentially the only bright spot on an otherwise drab year.

With dry theatrical humour Lachlan also takes us into the lives of ex-students, through the droll character of Dezzie in her checkout job at GOLO. This hysterical scene provides a glimpse into the lives of students who have dropped out and whose most exciting years are possibly already behind them; who stare in wonder as they encounter ex-teachers as customers with children—'Looks like he hates her' (p.32)—and are forced to consider that teachers may have some life outside school. Lachlan's informed observation is a damning indictment of so many state high schools staffed by teachers who 'never grow up because they never leave school so they never get a chance to go out into the real world' (p.63). Petchall at least represents teachers working within the system who care for their students—even if they are in danger of burnout.

Into this place of inertia and aimlessness comes a voice of remarkable energy, pace and rhythm: fifteen-year-old Tamara. Tamara is the student lurking at the back of many classrooms that shows some glimmer of potential, of talent; a writer in the making. She is also a smart-arse, quick-witted, with an incredible acerbic tongue. As the playground erupts into lockdown-drill chaos, Tamara wryly comments:

one girl looks like she is fuckin' shitting her sports daks (p.10)

Tamara observes the world around her and narrates it to us with rich detail and texture. At the same time we are acutely aware that she is only fifteen, and from the opening scene, that she is 'Three weeks, six days, seven hours' (p.3) into her first relationship—with Jasyn Donovan, aka 'Squid'. It is a relationship for which they have no positive role models, nor any guidance. Both mothers have shot through. Squid's follows random men around the country and Tamara's has left to start again with a new man of means. Over the course of the play we witness the inevitable destruction of this doomed first love. As appalling as it is, it feels inevitable, like a distant slow-motion car crash that we can neither prevent nor look away from. Lachlan masterfully divides the sympathies of the audience. Is any one person really to blame? Can one expect more or better for these young characters?

The first draft did not include the climactic classroom confrontation between Squid and Tamara. It was referred to but never seen. I felt as an audience we were being cheated of a great dramatic moment. I wanted to see Squid attacking Tamara about her devastating betrayal. With only a few references to what had occurred, Lachlan and I set up an improvisation with a group of gun actors to test whether our instincts for its inclusion were correct. In the highlight of our workshop we asked the actors to play out this moment. The public humiliation of Tamara in front of her class, having to accept her awful act of betrayal, is nothing less than tragic. What I didn't expect, and something which the actors so wonderfully evoked, was the sadness and vulnerability surrounding Squid. Devastated by Tamara's act he responds in the only way he knows how—by lashing out. The place of a teacher in this environment was also something of a revelation. Petchall also confronts the reality of Tamara's flawed character whilst trying to protect her and Squid from the consequences of his actions. Our sympathies are tugged in three ways and we are left gasping.

It is a credit to Lachlan that he managed to recreate so clearly the words, atmosphere and complex character motivations that played out in this improvisation and translate them into a succinct passage of text. But of course he had led the actors to this point with such well-crafted characters that in some ways it was obvious what was going to occur. Not to detract from Lachlan's ability, there is something so direct and powerful in, 'She's just a dumb slut who fucked your brother' (p.71) shockingly delivered from the mouth of a teacher, that one wonders if it could only be discovered through improvisation.

I concur with Alyson Campbell's statement that, 'Philpott's plays are connected by themes of love and loneliness, pierced with the idea that we can't know anyone fully and that, in the end, we are always alone'. Both Squid and Tamara 'try to do things right but they fuck up anyway'. Tamara's father, Laurence, is one of the play's most isolated and lonely characters. His wife, wanting more, has left him for Johan and 'her second-chance kids'. At first we have little sympathy for him. His racist slurs in front of Jasyn are cringeable and his lack of parental care for Tamara borders on neglect. We therefore don't judge Tamara's, 'Cragged-up old faggot. Hate him. What chance he give me?' (p.38), in fact we almost rally with her against him. However Lachlan's characters are always multi-faceted. The revelation of Laurence's HIV status changes the course of the play and the characters' behaviours. On one level it is a subtle commentary on the continuing presence of this disease in our society and on another, an exploration of the sexual identity of a man and father now perhaps exploring his options post-separation. The nurse's announcement to Tamara is as dreadful to her as it is to us. Who is this man? Did she ever know him? Tamara's ridiculous fear of catching the disease whilst living with her father reflect a society that should know better after thirty years, yet still demonstrates both ignorance and bigotry. The fact that Laurence's true sexual identity is never fully analysed or revealed is appropriate. As in his earlier play, *Bison*, Lachlan reminds us of the ongoing presence of HIV-AIDS in all our lives.

Ironically, the scene from which the play takes its title is the one genuine moment of connection between its lead characters. Dancing silently in a carnival tent, hooked up to iPods, Tamara and Squid experience one pure moment of happiness. Dancing face to face, listening to music selected by the other, separate and at the same time intensely together, it is a moment of sheer theatrical beauty:

> We face each other in the silent disco.
> I look at your eyes—your tough eyes aren't tough aren't hard they're smiling.
> Right there and then—everything else blown away—just you and me Squid.
> You so close I can feel you breathe. We've never danced like this before.
> You reach out and pull me closer to you. The way you pull me in—makes me feel like I'm the best thing in the world. (p.66)

Finally, I return to a recurring line from the play, 'wonder how I'll remember this'. Whether it be through pop songs, items of clothing, smells, books, a look or even a tattoo, the characters in *Silent Disco* let us know that regardless of the boredom, they understand the importance of this time in their lives, and that they will always remember it. This gently-woven theme of memory elevates the drama and invites us all to consider the course of our own lives. What more could one ask of any play?

Noel Jordan
February 2011

ACKNOWLEDGEMENTS

Silent Disco has been developed with the support of The Aurora Theatre Company, Australian Theatre for Young People (atyp), Griffin Theatre Company and Playwriting Australia. Thanks to each of these companies and to the artists who to have contributed to the development of this play. I would also like to make special acknowledgement to Alastair McKinnon for his encouragement, belief and support.

THANKS

Mark Adnum, Joshua Barnes, Jane Bodie, Wendy Buswell, Alyson Campbell, Elena Carapetis, Fraser Corfield, Katrina Douglas, Susannah Dowling, Eamon Farren, Kate Gaul, Tanika Gupta, Josh Hecht, Laura Hopkinson, Adele Jeffreys, Gary Jones and David Smith from Smith and Jones Management, Noel Jordan, Belinda Kelly, Ian Lawson, Lee Lewis, Nick Marchand, Michael Minten, Chris Mead, Luke Mullins, Penny Philpott, Jenny Rohr, Graham Matthew Smith, Jonathon Spector, Sam Strong, Elizabeth Surbey and Ben White.

Silent Disco was first produced by Griffin Theatre Company, atyp and HotHouse Theatre at the SBW Stables Theatre, Sydney, on 27 April 2011 with the following cast:

PETCHALL / DEZZIE / LEANNE / AUNTY	Camilla Ah Kin
TAMARA	Sophie Hensser
DANE / LAURENCE / TEACHER	Kirk Page
SQUID	Meyne Wyatt

Director, Lee Lewis
Designer, Justin Nardella
Lighting Designer, Ross Graham
Sound Designer / Composer, Stefan Gregory
Production Manager, Glenn Dulihanty

CHARACTERS

TAMARA BREWSTER
JASYN (SQUID) DONOVAN
DANE DONOVAN
HELEN PETCHALL
LAURENCE BREWSTER
TEACHER
DEZZIE
LEANNE
AUNTY

CASTING NOTE

The actor who plays Dane can also play Laurence and Teacher.
The actor who plays Helen can also play Dezzie, Leanne and Aunty.
If actors double in this manner they will render the voice of these
extra roles rather than attempting to embody them.

TEXT NOTE

/   indicates a point of interruption and/or overlap

SQUID/TAMARA indicates lines to be said simultaneously, with
    assignment of lines to correspond to placement of character's name

… indicates an unfinished sentence

[ ] bracketed words for actor's information, not delivery

STAGING NOTE: SOUND

Audience to be provided with earphones which deliver a soundtrack
more bearable than traffic, planes and school bells as well as the
perfect song for dancing—so perfect it annihilates anything else you
can hear, making you, even for the shortest time, dance with love in
your head and your heart and your eyes. And in your pants.

This play went to press before the end of rehearsals and may differ from
the play as performed.

ACT ONE

Around nine a.m., TAMARA *waits in an inner-city laneway. She listens to music on her earphones, seems transported to another place. She is meant to be in Petchall's classroom.*

SQUID *arrives.*

TAMARA: You took your time. Ya bring ya paint?

SQUID: Yeah.

TAMARA: Red?

SQUID: Yeah.

TAMARA: Good. Clash with her house. Teach her a lesson.

SQUID: What did she do?

TAMARA: Told ya. She rang the school 'n' dobbed on us for jigging. Now all the teachers are coming out here, checking the laneway. This'll shut her up.

   Do it. Like I said. Come on.

SQUID: Keep watch.

   SQUID *begins spraying 'DOG POUND' on the fence.*

TAMARA: I am. Hurry up.

   See her face when she comes out and finds this on her precious pink cement. Old bitch, sitting in there all day, she should get a life or die. The way she looks at me.

   Don't spell it wrong.

   Concentrate! Finish it. Go on.

   Fuck!

SQUID: What?

TAMARA: She's in there.

SQUID: She's not.

TAMARA: Blinds moved in the front window.

   SQUID *ducks down, hides.*

   A bell rings in the distance.

   Got ya.

PETCHALL: Move in quietly. You all know the rules, so show some manners.

Get them out of your ears. Now. Out. Earphones out.

How many times have I said this to you all?

I can still hear one. I'm waiting.

One.

Two.

Three/

TAMARA: Hurry up, you sped.

SQUID: Done. We going?

TAMARA: Get a pic first. Hold up your can/

SQUID: No.

TAMARA *takes a photograph of* SQUID *with her phone.*

PETCHALL: Silence. Just enjoy that for a moment.

TAMARA: Took it anyway.

SQUID: Delete it.

PETCHALL: Enjoy that quiet.

SQUID: We going or what?

PETCHALL: Honestly your ears'll turn to/

SQUID: What are you looking at me like that for? Going to class. Delete that pic or I'm dead.

SQUID *leaves.*

PETCHALL: If I see an earphone I will snip it. If any iPods make their way out, I will confiscate them.

I don't care about your rights or what your parents say.

A plane passes above.

TAMARA: Didn't think much of him at first looks a bit mean not like other guys I like bit mean tough but hot but something wrong something going on inside his head seeping out something strange not sick but weird then one day I see him and he looks different something nicer— dunno maybe he's just looking up 'stead of looking down. He smiles. That's what it is. He smiles at me.

SQUID *returns.*

SQUID: Rowney's at the end of the lane.

TAMARA: Late notes?

SQUID: Giving shit about uniforms.

TAMARA: Did he see you?

SQUID: Na.

TAMARA: Then/

SQUID: Might come down here.

TAMARA: Rowney?

SQUID: I'll go the other way.

TAMARA: Past the shop? Get me a Coke?
   Your shout?

SQUID: Na.

TAMARA: Go on. You're my boyfriend.

SQUID: No.

TAMARA: Three weeks, six days, seven hours.

SQUID: Not this again.

TAMARA: It matters.

SQUID: Matters to you.

   SQUID *smokes.*

TAMARA: Matters to you too, just don't know how to say nothing.
   You shouldn't smoke, not if you play footy, how you gonna run? Give
   us one.

SQUID: Can we get out of here?

TAMARA: What were you smiling at before?

SQUID: Smiling?

TAMARA: Yeah, coming back up the lane.

SQUID: Wasn't smiling.

TAMARA: You were. Whatever.
   Did ya win yesterday, Jasyn?

SQUID: No. Ref was shit.

TAMARA: Good excuse. School team sucks—bunch of weeds.

SQUID: Used to be good.

TAMARA: Yeah? When?

SQUID: Couple of years back. Before everyone left. My brother/

TAMARA: You don't talk about him much.

    I knew him.

SQUID: He's not dead.

TAMARA: Know him then. Dane.

    He looks like Sonny Bill Williams.

SQUID: Sonny Bill's a fag.

TAMARA: He still looks like your brother.

SQUID: He's a fucking Islander.

TAMARA: So?

SQUID: How you know Dane?

TAMARA: Seen him round. Out after footy. Not school footy. Proper footy on the weekend.

    He's hot. Better than you.

SQUID: You reckon?

TAMARA: Yeah.

SQUID: Thanks.

PETCHALL: Shaniqua… Dmitri… Jessica C…

TAMARA: No worries.

PETCHALL: Jessica F…

TAMARA: You visit Dane in jail?

PETCHALL: Jessica L…

SQUID: Yeah. No. Not allowed to *without adult supervision*.

TAMARA: Like a nightclub or something.

PETCHALL: Jessica P… oh sorry *Jess*.

SQUID: He didn't deal drugs.

TAMARA: No? He took them. Everyone said. That story about him and that footy slag after the grand final. That true?

SQUID: Wasn't there.

TAMARA: Yeah? Gotta be dumb to touch that shit. See what it does to people.

PETCHALL: Who's still missing then? Tamara Brewster? Tamara here?

SQUID: Delete the pic.

TAMARA: Make me.

    In a playful way, he does.

Between the bins in jiggers' lane things go still between us. We lean on bricks look at each other and something happens like in a movie. Like what happened when we were alone together for the first time. The traffic on the city bypass hushes.

We look at each other—into each other's…

[*To* SQUID] You've got something on your mouth. Not there, there.

SQUID: Is it gone?

Can I kiss you?

TAMARA: Na.

> *They kiss.*

PETCHALL: The AWOLs, the missing, the late ones, let's hope they turn up.

SQUID: You talk too much.

TAMARA: Three weeks, six days.

PETCHALL: Jasyn?/

SQUID: Of nonstop talk.

PETCHALL: Jasyn Donovan? Here?

SQUID: Can't believe you count.

TAMARA: It's 'cause *I can*.

Know how many days until the formal?

SQUID: Na.

TAMARA: Seventy-nine.

SQUID: Yeah right.

TAMARA: Hey Squid—thanks.

SQUID: For what?

TAMARA: Messing up the doghouse. Looks sick.

Go get me a Coke.

Zero. See you in class.

> *A bell rings.*

♦ ♦ ♦

TAMARA: English Six don't matter/ I'm late.

PETCHALL: You're late, Tamara.

TAMARA: No Miss, yes Miss.

She stands there in front of them all.

All of them in the same thing—blue shit 'cept/

PETCHALL: Where's your uniform today, Tamara?

TAMARA: Wearing it, Miss.

PETCHALL: That's what you call that, is it?

TAMARA: Kinda looks the same, Miss.

PETCHALL: Late note? Waiting.

TAMARA: She waits not for long/

PETCHALL: I'm waiting. I'm/ waiting…

TAMARA: … *waiting not for long*.

We know that, Miss. Lost my late note—can go and get one but then I'll miss more essential English Six.

PETCHALL: Sit down then.

TAMARA: We fuck about muck up swallow last crumbs of shit turn phones to silent hide 'em flick earphones inside collars turn them down real quiet drum beat's still there…

Boom boom/ boom boom.

PETCHALL: Tamara/

TAMARA: What now? Not doing nothing, Miss.

Boom boom boom boom on my neck turned right down quiet Kelly Blacklock yawns/

PETCHALL: Off now.

TAMARA: It is.

PETCHALL: It's not. It's/ on.

TAMARA: Off. God! Give me a break.

PETCHALL: Do you want to start the day at the Deputy's?

TAMARA: As if, Miss.

PETCHALL: Then/

TAMARA: Sorry Miss.

PETCHALL: Then/

TAMARA: Alright!

> *She makes a drama about turning her iPod off and putting her earphones away.*

Through the window bottom of a plane flies over school to land, Miss drowned out.

Kelly Blacklock's eyes shut—caffeine don't work—plane gone, Miss back/

PETCHALL: Your time as much as mine. So little time left until/

TAMARA: Miss points at black numbers on a whiteboard.

PETCHALL: … your *exam* and I trust you all remember the date.

      SQUID *enters.*

TAMARA: In he comes, in he comes looking like a rock star a football god shirt all tight round his arms.

PETCHALL: Ah Jasyn. Nearly forgotten what you looked like.

SQUID: Handsome, ay Miss?

PETCHALL: Sit down. Not there. Seating plan. Next to Phong.

TAMARA: Sucked in/ next to Phong.

PETCHALL: Kelly, what date is the exam?

TAMARA: Blankness empty nothing/

PETCHALL: Kelly!

TAMARA: Scares her wakes her turns her music down.

PETCHALL: Out of ears, Kelly. The exam date?

TAMARA: Surprise on her face, *exam*?

PETCHALL: Write it down this time, tattoo it on your brain if you can. Anyone? The exam date?

TAMARA: Nothing no-one nothing/

PETCHALL: The twenty-seventh. Diaries out? Diaries out. Write it down, write it down.

And why do you need to do the exam?

TAMARA: So we can get a job and leave our mark on the world, Miss.

PETCHALL: Good. Now.

Cast your minds back to what we did yesterday. Opinion. The importance of having an opinion and being able to express it?

I believe in arranged marriage.

TAMARA: Yawn/

PETCHALL: I think rugby league is for animals/

TAMARA: Mexican yawn/

PETCHALL: I think Fridays should be made into a weekend day/

TAMARA: Mexican yawn flying round the shit box.

PETCHALL: What about you? What do you think? Today you can crys-
  tallise your opinions because we are/ revising writing an opinion
  piece.

TAMARA: *Revising writing an opinion piece* all faces say the same.

PETCHALL: Too early in the morning to have an opinion, is it?

TAMARA: Don't ask me/

PETCHALL: Solomon, Ezekiel?/

TAMARA: Sitting like the living dead/

PETCHALL: Sol? Eze? You two awake? No? Who is/

TAMARA: Not me/

PETCHALL: Who would/ like to…

TAMARA: Anyone else not me/

PETCHALL: … come out the front and write/

TAMARA: No-one moves.

  Cement class.

  No-one does nothing.

  Plane overhead—Virgin Blue—Miss's voice swallowed up by/

PETCHALL: Tamara.

TAMARA: No.

PETCHALL: Yes. Kelly.

TAMARA: No.

PETCHALL: Yes. Have a pen each and come out and write something on
  the board.

TAMARA: Kelly? Write?

PETCHALL: Come on, you two.

TAMARA: Kelly, don't write—she rolls her eyes—looks down at her
  runners.

PETCHALL: Five things you have a strong opinion about. Now.

TAMARA: Oh Miss.

  We're out there in front of the others, me with Petchall's red marker
  Kelly with the black one for the tags 'n' shit on bus seats—cheeky
  bitch—not writing just looking at her—at Miss just looking Miss's
  way like/ this

SQUID: This is shit, Miss. Who cares about opinions? No-one gives a fuck
  about what we think.

PETCHALL: Thanks for sharing that language and that opinion, Jasyn. Now you two: five things you have a strong/ opinion about.

TAMARA: Girls, older girls slowly pass the window giggling, in no hurry carrying hoops 'n' shit/

SQUID: Hey Miss, can we do hula hoops?

TAMARA: They grease us through the window/

SQUID: Sluts/

TAMARA: Yeah, sluts/ with hoops

PETCHALL: No hoops, we can do opinion.

TAMARA: Why they doing hoops at school anyway? Like what do they reckon we are? Seals?

PETCHALL: Opinion, Tamara. Write!

TAMARA: Pen squeaks 1: h-a-t-/e.

SQUID/PETCHALL: Hate racists. Racism sucks.

TAMARA: 2.

Out the window last girl passing with a pink hoop, Kel writes fast./

SQUID/PETCHALL: Diet drinks suck.

TAMARA: I write: 3.

TAMARA/PETCHALL: Global warming sucks.

SQUID: 4.

SQUID/TAMARA: Immigration sucks.

PETCHALL: But/

TAMARA: Squid looking at me grinning winks—phone rings up the back Diana Filokostis groaning skank with big hair says Miss it's my sister really is Miss me mum's sick 'n' I need to take this call can I take it I gotta take it I'm going to take it I'm goin outside to take it I'll only be a… door slams.

Miss shrugs. She's looking out the window now. Up at the sky no plane right now just two clouds look like—two clouds look like/ two little monkeys.

PETCHALL: Two little monkeys.

Jasyn. Do you want to come up and have a go? Come and write something?/

TAMARA: He doesn't, clear he don't, he grips the desk swings back on the back two legs of the chair.

PETCHALL: Legs!

SQUID: Sorry Miss.

PETCHALL: Go on, have a go. Think about the world. When you look around what makes you angry? What gives you hope?

SQUID: Hope?

PETCHALL: Yes.

TAMARA: Formal dresses give me hope. A silver dress like a mirror and I'm inside it, dancing in the middle of the/ dance floor and—

A bell sounds in five long chilling rings.

PETCHALL: Lockdown.

TAMARA: Screams—horror film screams—outside inside.

SQUID: A lockdown, Miss?

TAMARA: Screams then silence and through the window/

SQUID: Miss?

TAMARA: See girls outside running back to E Block screaming
running back the way they came
running squealing hoops flying
look like they're having one big joke all running
na maybe they don't
faces aren't joking—look scared maybe
one girl looks like she's fuckin' shitting her sports daks
poor sluts running
then one of them stops—turns back stands planted into the ground
staring at something coming.
Still bitch. Colour all drained from the still bitch with the pink hoop./
Is it a drill?

SQUID: Is it a drill?

PETCHALL: I don't know. Everyone. Sit down.

TAMARA: Still bitch with the hoop stares straight ahead don't move.
What's she do, Miss? Her out there?

SQUID: She's locked out of the lockdown.

TAMARA: Miss moves towards the window stares out at her.
A wrapper flutters across the quad.
A pigeon glances from the ledge at hoop girl.

SQUID: Look at her.

PETCHALL: Don't look at her.

TAMARA: We look at her. Friends all gone—she's alone—she's still.

SQUID: What's going on?

TAMARA: Must be bad, hey Miss, if that they think it's safer in here with us?

SQUID: Gang with blades taking revenge for shit.

PETCHALL: For what?

TAMARA: Bomb scare? Some freaky Muslim?

SQUID: They're all freaky.

PETCHALL: That's enough.

TAMARA: Canteen ladies with rifles after her 'cause she scabs 'n' shit.

SQUID: Why are we locked in? Why'd them girls run across the playground like some pedo was/

PETCHALL: We have to stay in here until the bell sounds again.

TAMARA: Class groans. Still girl in the quad starts moving—shouting, she hits at the office doors—bangs on the window—she's gonna break the glass, Miss, look on her face is fear—panic.

SQUID: I'll go out and protect her, Miss.

TAMARA: Then there's a shadow, a man.

SQUID: Pedo.

TAMARA: Man walking towards her—she's got nowhere to/ go.

SQUID: It's Rowney.

TAMARA: Rowney!

SQUID: Pedo!

PETCHALL: Jasyn!

TAMARA: Rowney in his Principal suit with his master keys rottweiler eyes—

SQUID: He's escaped, that's why they rang the bell.

TAMARA: Rowney points at the girl, shakes his head and she starts to crumble, she's crying like something bad went down—like she really got attacked—stupid bitchface princess.

PETCHALL: Time to get on with some work.

TAMARA: Rowney picks up the hoop.

Unlocks the door.

Leads her back inside.

PETCHALL: Pens out.

SQUID: Oh Miss, can't we go?

PETCHALL: Not until they let us know.

TAMARA: Typical.

SQUID/TAMARA: Beep beep/

PETCHALL: Who was that?

TAMARA: sms

SQUID: let's get out right now?

PETCHALL: Put it away.

SQUID: Beep beep

PETCHALL: Off.

SQUID: sms

TAMARA: like how dickhead?

PETCHALL: Whose was that? I will confiscate those,

> *A bell rings.*

There you go. It was a drill.

TAMARA: That sucks.

PETCHALL: Thanks everyone, you may go.

Jasyn?

SQUID: Yes Miss?

PETCHALL: May we talk a moment?

SQUID: It's recess, Miss.

PETCHALL: I know. Just wanted to say… It's been a while.

SQUID: Yes Miss.

PETCHALL: It's good to see you're back. Where have you been?

SQUID: Dunno.

PETCHALL: You're back now? You're going to come to class? Get your School Certificate?

SQUID: Of course, Miss.

PETCHALL: Good. It's not too late you know. With a bit of work you could do well. If you need some help.

SQUID: Yes Miss/

PETCHALL: To catch up. Come and see me.

SQUID: Yes Miss, that all?

PETCHALL: Yes.

> SQUID *goes.*

> *A plane.*

Classroom E19, the motley blue plastic chairs, leaky gas heater, graffiti on desktops and underneath chewing gum relief maps of teen angst and restlessness. Tired poster of Jane Austen on the back wall—all teeth blacked out and a Hitler moustache—the only pair of eyes that bother looking.

iPods off.

Pens out books open eyes to the front—to the…

I watch them. We all watch them. See—something untucked, some arm cut some name in marker on some hand. And in their eyes…

Willing with integrity. On the crest of the uniform. The school motto. 'Willing with integrity'. Nobody knows what that means.

Tamara's house.

TAMARA: Squid at my place—standing in the kitchen doorway staring out at the broken shit in the backyard.

> Dad looking at him—saying/

LAURENCE: Squid. What's his real name?

TAMARA: Ask him yourself.

LAURENCE: Squid your real name?

SQUID: No.

TAMARA: What's your real name then?

SQUID: Jasyn.

LAURENCE: Jasyn.

SQUID: Yeah. What's *your* real name?

LAURENCE/TAMARA: Laurence.

SQUID: Laurence.

LAURENCE: Of Arabia/

TAMARA: Not/

SQUID: What?

TAMARA: Don't worry, he'll go to his room soon.

LAURENCE: Nice.

TAMARA: Dinner's in five.

SQUID/LAURENCE: What is it?

TAMARA: Macaroni. We're not havin' salad—so don't ask—nothing to make it with—you want it—you find something to make it with—can Squid stay?

LAURENCE: For dinner?

TAMARA: Yeah.

LAURENCE: Stay over?

TAMARA: /Yeah.

LAURENCE: No.

TAMARA: Why not? Fuckin' hell. What do ya reckon we'll do?

What do you reckon we'll…

What'll you know anyway?

Don't worry he won't know—won't hear us from the front room.

LAURENCE: You reckon?

TAMARA: *God!* We're just gonna watch a DVD.

Then he starts acting like a dad. First time in fifteen years saying/

LAURENCE: So what do you do with yourself, Jasyn?/ And where do you live?

TAMARA: And where do you live? See his uniform—he goes to school with me—and where you reckon he lives?

LAURENCE: You won't be convincing her to stay on at school then.

TAMARA: What does that mean?

'Cause of the colour of his skin?

Right.

Thank fuck I missed the racist sexist moron genes.

LAURENCE: I didn't/ [mean that]

TAMARA: I'm staying on. Don't need no convincing from a bloke. Not going to leave school and work in some shithouse two-dollar shop for the rest of my life—get varicose veins standing up all day selling fucked-up stuffed shit to cheapskates.

You reckon I'm going to have people sneer down at me like I got not brain?

I'm going to be a writer.

LAURENCE: A writer?

TAMARA: Yeah a writer. Kids' books. Some parents read to their kids.

LAURENCE: Lots of money in that.

TAMARA: There is.

LAURENCE: You can get your mate here to do the pictures. Dot paintings.

TAMARA: Tea's ready. You need sauce? If you do we're out.

LAURENCE: Dry macaroni?

TAMARA: Dribble on it.

> He takes his plate away to the front room—door ajar but he's gone, that's it—there's a canyon between us now and for the first time ever I'm glad.
>
> That's Laurence.

SQUID: He sick?

TAMARA: In the fucking head. Sorry. About/

SQUID: No I mean/

TAMARA: Sick. Na.

SQUID: He looks/

TAMARA: What?

SQUID: Nothing.

TAMARA: He's a fucking freak. Hides out in his room like a spider.

SQUID: What's he do in there?

TAMARA: Watches sci-fi shit, I dunno.

> Him and Mum hate each other—reckons it's a big joke she works for Virgin, not that she gets to fly in the planes—not pretty enough. She's not.
>
> Both spend their lives on their arses watching things fly.
>
> You stare at the thing with strings and nails hanging on the wall.

SQUID: What's that thing do?

TAMARA: Do? Nothing. Just some ugly shit Dad made at school. He put it up when Mum left.

> He went to our school, you know—way before laptops and the internet—probably the same teachers.
>
> Reckons AC/DC came to play.

SQUID: No.

TAMARA: Yeah.

SQUID: Why?

TAMARA: Felt sorry for them. Na, they won some competition. AC/DC played three songs—teachers must have hated every second of it—bet they kept the bad kids out.

SQUID: They always do.

Anything else to eat?

TAMARA: Na. What you want to do?

SQUID: What's your dad got to drink?

TAMARA: Drink? Dad doesn't drink anything. Not even water. There might be something in the cupboard from... Mum used to drink bourbon.

SQUID: Nothing here.

TAMARA: No.

SQUID: Get something—shop's still open.

What do you want?

TAMARA: Don't have cash.

He holds up fifty dollars.

SQUID: Got this. We can have whatever we want.

PETCHALL: We used to have discos, when deejays played records and kids actually danced. Girls with lipstick and blush—first kiss at the disco—slicked-back boys with nasty cologne who'd look away and say *You wanna dance, Miss?*

TAMARA: Creep past Laurence watching his alien shit *I'm walking Jasyn home* past Jerry next door staring off at the gutter like it's some ocean view—wish we had somewhere good to go.

PETCHALL: Deaf girl. Jane Spitteri. Came to all the discos. Said even though she couldn't hear the music she loved the beat. That song—*the only way is up for you baby*. The way she danced to that song. I'll never forget it.

TAMARA: You swipe it from Subway?

SQUID: Didn't swipe it.

TAMARA: They got cameras, you know.

Where'd you get it?

SQUID: What's it matter?

TAMARA: Just want to know.

PETCHALL: 'Living on a Prayer', 'Girls Just Wanna Have Fun', 'Let's Go Crazy'…

TAMARA: Tell me, Jasyn.

SQUID: Don't want to.

PETCHALL: I want to dance, I want to feel the heat.

SQUID: Want something to eat? Drink?

PETCHALL: I want to dance with somebody—with somebody who loves me.

TAMARA: Tell me where you got the money.

PETCHALL: Words and dances everyone knew. The Nutbush, The Time Warp, then parents picking up their kids, thanking us for/

TAMARA: You wink and step into the grog shop come back with/

SQUID *with a bottle of Beam.*

SQUID: Want some?

TAMARA: Tell me where you got the money.

SQUID: Found a wallet. Big deal. Have some.

TAMARA: I'm okay.

SQUID: Go on. Peer pressure.

TAMARA: No.

SQUID: Go on.

TAMARA: Got an English test tomorrow/

SQUID: *Got an English test tomorrow.* So?

PETCHALL: I put novels on their desks *Anne of Green Gables*, *Pride and Prejudice*, *The Secret Garden*, *A Patch of…* Open those ratty old text books. Look past the stains at the names in the list on the inside front cover. Open them up. Look at that list. The people who have had to carry that book around before you got it. All the boys and girls who were expected to read these stories… How many did? How many started? How many finished because…

TAMARA: You study for it?

SQUID: Yeah.

TAMARA: Right. You'll fail.

SQUID: Yeah.

TAMARA: All the teachers expect/

SQUID: What?

TAMARA: They expect you to fail so why don't you/ [try?]

SQUID: What?

TAMARA: Nothing.

> *They are at the park.*

The park—dark and dead quiet. Fig trees stretch out arms. Circle of bottles and shit left on the grass—hot chips gone cold—dog barking—shut up ya mutt!

Fruit bat above disappears in a cloud.

Going to rain maybe.

SQUID: No.

TAMARA: Will.

SQUID: Won't.

TAMARA: Can smell it.

SQUID: No.

TAMARA: Dark, isn't it? No stars.

> TAMARA *watches* SQUID *for a while.*

You know what I used to think of you? Like when I first saw you?

SQUID: Na.

TAMARA: Thought you were scary. You looked mean. I wondered if you ever smiled. Used to watch you in class and shit. See if you'd smile.

SQUID: Did I?

TAMARA: Na.

SQUID: Hate school.

TAMARA: Yeah, but you gotta get through.

Bat above us lands in the fig tree.

Hate Tuesdays.

SQUID: Better then Mondays.

TAMARA: No. Tuesdays suck.

SQUID: What do you mean?

TAMARA: Bad shit always happens Tuesdays.

SQUID: Like what?

TAMARA: You really want to know?

SQUID: Yeah.

TAMARA: Mum left on a Tuesday.

Ran off with this Dutch wanker. Tuesday the twentieth of March. My birthday.

Dad stopped work on a Tuesday. See? Na.

SQUID: What day did we meet?

TAMARA: Wednesday.

SQUID: No.

TAMARA: Yeah.

SQUID: No. I'd been at sport. Was a Tuesday.

TAMARA: Was a Tuesday.

Something moves in the bushes behind them, screeches, flutters into the night.

SQUID: What the fuck? Scare you?

TAMARA: Na. A bit.

SQUID: Scared me.

TAMARA: Did it?

SQUID: Na.

TAMARA: Things stop.

Nothing.

Just us.

Just you and me.

Why they call you Squid?

SQUID: Told ya that.

TAMARA: But you didn't tell me the story.

SQUID: No.

TAMARA: Why?

SQUID: Don't remember it.

TAMARA: Is it from the dreamtime?

SQUID *laughs.*

SQUID: It's just a story Mum made up.

TAMARA: Hate this park—just a fucking dog toilet.

SQUID: Used to be nice.

TAMARA: Yeah? When?

SQUID: Used to come here when I was a kid. With my mum and brothers.

TAMARA: Yeah?

SQUID: Seemed much bigger then.

TAMARA: Everything from when you were a kid seems bigger.

And better, ay? Before things went to the shitter.

Where's your mum, Squid?

She looks up and holds her palms open to the sky.

It's spitting, dickhead, look.

Told you it would, you fucking clueless cockhead…

I look back and you are crying.

A tear on your cheek.

You? Squid? Jasyn? Crying?

I want to outline the tear trailing down your face with a pen so I don't forget it. Don't know what to say. You blink—look straight ahead—don't know if you know I noticed.

SQUID: What?

He reaches for TAMARA*'s hand squeezes it.*

TAMARA: Nothing.

Your hand lets mine go

runs up my leg

opens buttons

squeezes inside

taste of salt from your cheeks on my tongue.

We kiss—your tongue in my mouth licking around inside it and you push me down on the grass it's soft and wet

hands gentle to start and then you lift up my t-shirt unzip my jeans cold air and your warm hands against my skin.

I'm lying on the grass in the dark looking up at the sky—the dark—like ink all around me getting deeper and deeper this ink splashing staining me—I cannot breath down here/

SQUID: You okay?

TAMARA: Yeah.

SQUID: Kiss me.

They kiss for a moment.

TAMARA: Up the top where the light is, it's a long way above me.

Struggle to get free to get to the top.

What holds me there is you. Your arms reach out, touch me, hold me keep me there.

Gently, but they do.

Your hands press me—your breath pins me.

And I need to let go, I need to breathe, need to be here with you, stop pushing back.

I stop pushing back, stop thinking and sink down into the ink. The ink is velvet and the lights at the top are a long way away now.

SQUID: You okay?

Pause.

TAMARA: Happened quick.

SQUID: What do you mean?

TAMARA: Just.

SQUID: Didn't. You okay?

TAMARA: Stop asking that.

SQUID: You okay?

TAMARA: Just said yes.

SQUID: Did it?

TAMARA: What?/ Hurt?

SQUID: Hurt?

TAMARA: No.

SQUID: Was it?

TAMARA: What?

SQUID: Your first time?

TAMARA: Was it yours?

They look at each other searching for how to treat the other.

SQUID: Need a piss.

He goes to piss.

A truck roars past.

TAMARA: Nice but not that nice.

Hurts but doesn't hurt much as much as I thought it would.

Rain stops. For the first time I notice I'm wet all over—my hair stuck to my face my clothes stuck to me—can hear myself breathing. Wonder how I will remember this.

As SQUID *returns he zips his trousers up and sits next to* TAMARA *but not as close as before. They drink Beam.*

Do you love me?

Nothing.

Squid?

SQUID: Maybe.

TAMARA: Maybe?

SQUID: It hasn't been that long.

TAMARA: Maybe? It's been four weeks.

SQUID: Do you love me?

TAMARA: Na.

TAMARA *goes.*

PETCHALL: You never realise it and they are walking out your door. Jane Spitteri what happened to her? And Suzie Furlong. Skinny Suzie Furlong. Ballet shoes dangling off her bag. Smiled a lot and stared into space, then… walked out one Tuesday for the last time.

Shanice Whoppapwhago. Part-time job at the fruit market check-out on the weekends then Mondays, then Tuesday's too, then… I still have her 'This Is My Life' assignment. She left school before I could give back. Sitting in unclaimed marking on my desk—her smiling in the photo she stuck on the front. This is your life, Shanice. Suzie. Jane.

It rains.

◆ ◆ ◆

SQUID *visits* DANE *in prison.*

DANE: How did you get here?

SQUID: Walked.

DANE: Walked?

SQUID: From the bus stop.

DANE: Didn't think they let you in.

SQUID: Na. [*He whispers.*] Got ID.

DANE: They give you hard time?

SQUID: Not really.

DANE: Good. Where did you get your ID?

SQUID: Made it.

DANE: Show me.

   No. Just hold it up.

   Nice.

SQUID: Thanks.

DANE: You the same age as me, then? We twins?

SQUID: Maybe. Yeah.

> *They look at each other for a long time.*

   So.

DANE: So what?

SQUID: How you doing?

DANE: You know.

SQUID: Na.

DANE: How could you?

SQUID: What do you mean?

DANE: Been here two years? What's this, your second visit?

> *Long pause.*

   What's happening out there? How're the boys doing?

SQUID: Alright.

DANE: That's it?

SQUID: Yeah.

DANE: They beat those wankers from north side?

> SQUID *shrugs.*

   Who's playing five-eight, then?

SQUID: Dunno.

DANE: What?

SQUID: Don't know, Dane. Not going. Think about it.

   Can't go. Can I?

> *Pause.*

DANE: Do you have a girl? You're what—fourteen?

     SQUID *grimaces.*

  You got a girl?

SQUID: Yeah.

DANE: Get into her pants? Do you?

  Bet you do. When I was your age…

  Cry.

SQUID: What?

DANE: Cry. They love it. Not all the time, just now and then. Bawl in a movie or hold her hand and look up at the moon and cry.

  Bitches go mad for that shit.

  What's her name?

SQUID: Tamara.

DANE: She pretty?

SQUID: *No*, she's a dog. Of course she is.

DANE: She smart?

SQUID: Yeah.

DANE: You really like her, don't you?

SQUID: She's alright.

DANE: You love her?

SQUID: Why you asking me all this shit?

DANE: You're my bro.

SQUID: You heard from Mum, Dane?

     DANE *laughs.*

DANE: Have you?

SQUID: You remember the story she used to tell us about the squid?

DANE: The only thing I remember her telling is lies.

    Pause.

  Tamara, hey?

  Can't wait to meet her.

SQUID: Not bringing her here.

DANE: Not going to be here forever.

SQUID: You coming out?

DANE: How's Aunty? She still play cricket with you in the street in the ad breaks?

SQUID: You coming out?

DANE: 'Course I'm coming out. Things'll be just like they used to be.

SQUID: Like they used to be?

DANE: Yeah.

> SQUID *doesn't look at* DANE.

SQUID: Aunty hasn't done anything like that since we were kids. You've forgotten what it's like.

I gotta go.

> SQUID *leaves but doesn't know where to go. He stands alone, listens to his iPod.*

♦ ♦ ♦

TAMARA *reads.*

TAMARA: Dark ink and if I lie in it, if I let myself fall back into it—it'll stain me—I'll look different when I get to the top. I want to get to the top where the light is. I'm a long way down, don't want to get stained but something holds me stops me pushes me down? Struggle to get free but I can't. Am I drowning? What holds me there is him—his massive pulsating pink tentacles push me down into the ink.

PETCHALL/TAMARA: Until I know, until I accept I'm…

PETCHALL: … staying below forever in the dark.

It's very good, Tamara.

TAMARA: Why'd you keep me after class to read it?

PETCHALL: What inspired you to write it?

TAMARA: *That's why.* Nothing.

PETCHALL: If there's anything/ you like to talk about.

TAMARA: Oh Miss, it's just a dumb story about an octopus.

PETCHALL: Is it?

> TAMARA *rolls her eyes.*

It's not dumb, Tamara, it's… moving.

Would you like to type it up for the *Gazette*?

TAMARA *sighs.*

Wouldn't take you long.

TAMARA: Dunno.

PETCHALL: Do you have time?

TAMARA: I dunno.

PETCHALL: It's just really… imaginative.

Would you mind if I did?

TAMARA: No.

PETCHALL: You wouldn't mind or you don't want me to, which? Do you want people to read it?

TAMARA: Nobody reads the *Gazette*, Miss.

PETCHALL: I'll type it up anyway.

And how are things with you?

TAMARA: What do you mean?

The bell rings.

PETCHALL: Not a trick question, Tamara. Just asking how things are.

TAMARA: Alright.

PETCHALL: Good. Are you going to go to the formal?

TAMARA: Dunno.

PETCHALL: You should. It'll be fun.

TAMARA: Suppose.

PETCHALL: A slinky dress and a hot date.

TAMARA: Miss!

PETCHALL: It's all the girls talk about, isn't it? Their dresses and their hair and/

TAMARA: Miss?

PETCHALL: Yes Tamara.

TAMARA: It isn't my best one. I have better stories than that. It was for a test and Tanya had her iPod on and it was shit 'cause it was wrecking my concentration… but I could bring them in. Other ones?

PETCHALL: Of course. I'd love to read them.

TAMARA: I want to write kids books. Mum used to read to me in bed.

PETCHALL: Being read to is wonderful, isn't it?

TAMARA: Can I go now, Miss?

PETCHALL: But bring them in, the stories, don't…

TAMARA: Yes Miss.

TAMARA goes.

A plane takes off.

PETCHALL: Brittany Maycomb. Policeman's daughter, laugh like a burglar alarm in the middle of the night. Got pregnant in Year Nine. Left to have the baby. Could've stayed but… Jade Walters. Crazy girl. Couldn't stop her talking. Like something wound too tight. Then one day, Jade stopped smiling, started losing weight so fast she just faded. Faded out the school gate.

♦ ♦ ♦

SQUID *waits, wearing earphones.* TAMARA *sees him at a distance.*

TAMARA: He's waiting out the front now I like that Jasyn's waiting. I like that he's there at the gate waiting for me. When he sees me he'll smile from the side of his mouth look on his face says he hasn't been in class all day smells like it too, smells like he's been jigging one earphone in my ear the other in his…

They kiss.

SQUID: There's gonna be a fight.

TAMARA: Who?

SQUID: Thahn and Gary.

TAMARA: Thahn? That slaphead.

SQUID: Don't call him that.

TAMARA: The chink then. Who's Gary?

SQUID: Sped with the big ears.

TAMARA: Oh.

SQUID: *Hi, I'm Gary, what you doing?*

TAMARA: Oh him. Why're they fighting?

SQUID: Dunno.

TAMARA: Big deal—a chink and a sped. Who cares who wins.

SQUID: Gary'll kill him, but. Spastics are strong.

TAMARA: I want a smoke.

SQUID: No time.

TAMARA: Easy for you—I just had double English.

SQUID: It's Gary. It'll be a laugh.

TAMARA: Don't want to. Hate that shit.

SQUID: It'll be sick. Film it, put it online. Come on.

TAMARA: No.

SQUID: Come on.

TAMARA: Stampede. Nothing like that the fuckin' belting beat of three hundred kids bolting to see two smash each other up—watching it with the music full pelt phones filming it ready to upload.

SQUID: You filming?

TAMARA: Yeah.

SQUID: Chink hasn't got a chance.

TAMARA: He ducks and runs away each time Gary gets close. Circle of kids moves in and there's nowhere for him to run everyone screaming…

SQUID: … leading the chanting…

SQUID/TAMARA: *Gary Gary Gary Gary!*

TAMARA: In the nose the nose the nose side of the head the guts.

SQUID: Ooohhh. Look at the blood. Fucking mad.

TAMARA: Slap's over on his side in dirt getting punched in the gut in the gut in the gut.

SQUID: He's down.

SQUID/TAMARA: Teachers!

TEACHER: Get on your way.

Move on right now. You ought to be ashamed of yourselves.

Move on now. All of you. Go!

TAMARA: Fucking teachers ruin everything, don't they?

SQUID: Fucked-up real bad.

TAMARA: The chink?

SQUID: Yeah. Thahn.

TAMARA: How do you spell that?

SQUID: What?

TAMARA: His name. How do you/ spell it?

SQUID: What's it matter?

It was sick. Did you get it on your phone?

TAMARA: Yeah.

SQUID: Can I watch?

TAMARA: No. Fuck off!

SQUID: What's wrong?

TAMARA: Thahn. Don't get it. He wasn't even fighting back. He couldn't win. Why did he want to fight?

SQUID: Want to fight?

TAMARA: All the time with his arms by his side like…

Made me want to see him really hurt. Wanted him to get fucked-up bad.

What's wrong with us?

SQUID: What do you mean?

TAMARA: All that blood—the way we cheered when he hit the ground. What's wrong with us?

SQUID: There's nothing wrong with us. You okay?

TAMARA: Why you always fucking ask me that? *You okay? You okay?* I wasn't in the fucking fight.

SQUID: You just seem…

TAMARA: Deal with it.

SQUID: Want to go?

TAMARA: Yeah.

What you following me for?

SQUID: I…

TAMARA: What? Finish what you say for once, Jase.

SQUID: Never get a chance.

TAMARA: I'm gonna go.

SQUID: Can I come to yours?

TAMARA: Why?

SQUID: Just…

TAMARA: Gotta go to work.

SQUID: Can I/

TAMARA: What?/

SQUID: Don't bother.

TAMARA: Why don't we ever go to yours?

Pause.

Why don't we ever go to yours?

SQUID: It's shit.

TAMARA: Never seen it.

SQUID: It's shit, that's why. Don't want you to see it.

TAMARA: Your mum there?

SQUID: No.

TAMARA: Where is she?

> *Pause.*

Used to think Mary was your mum.

SQUID: Who?

TAMARA: You know, Mary. Sleeps outside 7-Eleven. The cranky one, bitch with the bags. Always scabbing change—drunk and shit.

> *Pause.*

SQUID: Funny.

TAMARA: Shit. Sorry. That was/

SQUID: Maybe she is.

TAMARA: I was joking, Jase.

SQUID: Well it was really funny.

TAMARA: I didn't mean nothing.

SQUID: Yes you did. What'd you say that for? Honest.

TAMARA: I don't know. Guess I shouldn't have. I didn't mean…

I got to get to work.

Squid?

SQUID: What?

TAMARA: Come over later?

> SQUID *stands on the street and watches her leave. He puts in his earphones.*

DANE: Don't talk about Amanda much but she is pretty. Doesn't look like other mothers. Real pretty—everyone says it—and Aunty says she knows it too—that's what the problem's always been.

Amanda made choices. Left us behind in her shadow, chose to be with men. Followed them. Send a letter north and it gets returned then she rings you from the south. She went south for Rory, west for Ron, north for Mick. Followed them—left us. Never said nothing—just wasn't there no more and when people ask why—we say nothing too. Nothing to say about that.

SQUID *goes.*

♦ ♦ ♦

TAMARA *at the GOLO discount store.*

TAMARA: Thursday night. Fluoro lights buzz—Elton John for the third fucking time in two hours—hate him, depressing old fuck—stuck on the register.

Washing powder in big boxes walking out the door and fake sheepskin ugg boots, Dezzie's got the shits.

What time you on till, Dezzie?

Dezzie?

sms fight with her boyfriend, manager's on another break—slobbing in the food court.

Indian woman with three young kids staring at me so I turn my back.

Two hours ten minutes left.

Hag behind me asking if we sell jam.

Jam? I dunno.

Dezzie. We sell jam?

DEZZIE: Dunno.

TAMARA: We dunno.

You go to your formal, Dezzie?

DEZZIE: Yeah.

TAMARA: Where was it?

DEZZIE: Some rusty boat. Went round and round the same bit of water while they played shit eighties music. Fed us burnt rissoles. There was a coleslaw fight, got on the dresses.

TAMARA: Coleslaw?

DEZZIE: Yeah.

TAMARA: You still vego?

DEZZIE: Yeah. Na.

TAMARA: Did you make up with ya boyfriend?

DEZZIE: Na.

TAMARA: You miss school, Dezzie?

DEZZIE: Na.

TAMARA: How do you cope working here full-time, doesn't it shit you?

DEZZIE: Can't be bothered looking for another job. Was going to sell this organic make-up like what Natalie Bassingthwaighte wears. Really good commission.

TAMARA: Commission?

DEZZIE: Yeah.

TAMARA: What happened?

DEZZIE: They gave me some to take home and try and it gave me a rash.

TAMARA: Maths teacher from school in the shop. Look, it's Mrs Brain. That her son?

DEZZIE: Looks like her—the chin and shit.

TAMARA: Looks like he hates her.

DEZZIE: He hates her for sure.

TAMARA: *Hello Tamara, Dezzie* she says.

DEZZIE/TAMARA: Hi Miss.

TAMARA: How do they do that? Know names?

Her kid looks away. His mum being called Miss. 'Cause she's not—a Miss. That's for someone younger, nicer.

Some smell. Some perfume she's wearing something reminds me of my mum—Dezzie serving her, me staring at her kid, he's pretty ugly big and weird—all in black—some emo loser.

DEZZIE: See the look she gave us? Teachers are bitches.

TAMARA: Some are okay.

DEZZIE: No they're not. Did you see his arm?

TAMARA: No.

DEZZIE: Had a cut on it, here.

TAMARA: What you doing looking at his arms?

DEZZIE: You reckon he cuts himself?

TAMARA: Don't care, ay?

DEZZIE: Yeah, but.

TAMARA: You ever go shopping with your mum?

DEZZIE: My mum?

TAMARA: Last time Mum and me went shopping she bought me these boots with tassels. Loved them. I wouldn't be seen dead anywhere with her now but I wish I still had the boots. Wonder where they are.

DEZZIE: Tassels are for sluts.

Pause.

TAMARA: Hate shopping centres. Hate the music and the smell of donuts everywhere. Hate how shit everyone looks under the lights all the pimples showing how you never know if it's night or day in them.

DEZZIE: He looked suicidal.

Wonder if she's strict at home? I had her in Year Nine. She was a full-on bitch. Wonder if she lets him listen to music and do Facebook 'n' shit or if it's all…

TAMARA: All what?

DEZZIE: Dunno.

TAMARA: Our formal's in the city at a restaurant near the harbour.

DEZZIE: Better than a shitty boat.

TAMARA: Yeah. Formal committee lied to the owner. Told him we're Year Twelves.

DEZZIE: Killer.

TAMARA: I want to go to the formal. Want to get a hot dress and shit but Squid doesn't want to go.

DEZZIE: Why not?

TAMARA: Dunno.

DEZZIE: Why do you call him that?

TAMARA: Squid?

DEZZIE: What's his real name?

TAMARA: Jasyn Donovan.

DEZZIE: No? Jasyn Donovan?

TAMARA: Yeah. Just happens I guess, like slutty girls called Brittany. Anyway he reckons it's a rip-off.

DEZZIE: His name?

TAMARA: No. The formal. Something to look forward to, but.

DEZZIE: Yeah, something to look forward to.

They stare into space.

♦ ♦ ♦

SQUID: Get home. Aunty looks at me funny.

> What's wrong? I done something? I haven't done something? What?/
> It's good news.

AUNTY/DANE: It's good news/

SQUID: She says. Good news. What is it, then?

> If it's so good why don't you say it straight away? If it's so good why
> you turn back to the telly, not say what the good news is?

AUNTY/DANE: Look at this idiot/

SQUID: She always says that/

DANE: Points to the telly shakes her head and mumbles/

AUNTY/SQUID/DANE: Look at this idiot.

AUNTY/DANE: Hasn't got a hope in hell.

SQUID: What's the news, Aunty?

DANE: I'm coming out.

SQUID: If it's good news why you still all quiet, Aunty?

SQUID/DANE: Aunty?

SQUID: You visit him every week, look into his eyes, you can't forget
> what it was like.

DANE: They still yell at each other next door?

AUNTY/SQUID: Don't talk like that.

DANE: Still play that fucking shitty trance music all weekend?

AUNTY/SQUID: Don't talk like that. He's your brother/ *Don't talk like
> that. He's your brother.*

DANE: Aunty still gets annoyed every Thursday 'cause everything she
> bought got eaten straight away?

> Remember that day Aunty cut her foot on the beer bottle all that
> brown glass in the soles of her feet?

> Blood footprints all the way up the hall?

> Must have hurt but she didn't swear or nothing.

> Never heard her swear. Not even the day I told her what I done.

SQUID/DANE: Good news, Aunty?

DANE: Isn't it?

SQUID/DANE: He's coming home./ I'm coming home.

PETCHALL: Weekend conference. Professional association. Try-hard
> teachers who take notes at a two-star hotel near Central, friands,

endless cups of stewed coffee. Last session on Sunday, most of the teachers shot off already. Last session of the day is called 'Challenging students—keeping them there—making it real'. Giving them a chance to make something of themselves believe in them more than their mothers.

◆ ◆ ◆

TAMARA *is in her room. She has her iPod in and dances like a possessed teenage slut.* SQUID *appears in her doorway and watches her for a while. She suddenly becomes aware of him.*

TAMARA: What the fuck do you think you're doing?

SQUID: I…

TAMARA: Reckon it's okay to barge in and spy on me, do you?

SQUID: Your dad let me in. Needed to…

TAMARA: What?

SQUID: Talk.

TAMARA: Yeah right. Fuck off.

SQUID: I wasn't spying.

TAMARA: You heard me. Fuck off, Jasyn.

SQUID: But…

TAMARA: Get out. Fuck off.

SQUID *stays in the doorway.* TAMARA *whacks him in the head.*

SQUID: Shit. What you do that for?

TAMARA: You deserve it. You don't get nothing, do you?

SQUID: Sorry.

TAMARA: What for? Bet you don't even know.

SQUID: For wrecking your privacy.

Pause.

TAMARA: Yeah. For wrecking me fucking privacy.

SQUID: What were you listening to?

TAMARA: Fuck off. What do you want?

SQUID: Want to ask you something.

TAMARA: Go on then.

SQUID: Don't hit me again.

> TAMARA *rolls her eyes.*

Will you/

TAMARA: What? Stop stuttering like a spaz.

SQUID: Will you go to the formal with me?

TAMARA: Thought you didn't want to go.

SQUID: Changed my mind.

TAMARA: You said *it's gonna be shithouse, waste me money.*

SQUID: I know.

TAMARA: So?

SQUID: I want to go. With you.

TAMARA: I'll think about it. You better piss off now. Dad'll hear us and go mental.

SQUID: But he let me in. Need to talk…

You don't want to hang out?

TAMARA: No.

> SQUID *exits.* TAMARA *puts on her iPod again.*

◆ ◆ ◆

PETCHALL: Staffroom—wait in line for the phone—endless ring at the other end—Wendy waiting next to me—tapping a pen clicking her tongue. Voice saying hello—faint at the other end—hello is this Mrs Donovan? It's Helen Petchall from the school? I'm ringing about Jasyn—Wendy tapping her watch pointing at the door. I'm ringing to say… It's good to see him back. No that's all. It's just… I thought we'd lost him.

Staff meeting—staff sitting, sighing, sweating hot afternoon the usual carnivals, raffle tickets, footy tipping, plans for morning teas, detention rosters, clock watching, fed rep counting seconds till we're free just like the kids and then I'm meant to report back on the conference meant to summarise two days in two minutes.

Then I get passed over till next meeting. *Sorry Helen but we need to do general business*—a question about the fights, how they've escalated, about fights and the change in the kids, have you noticed? Let's cancel things, teach them things add up, cancel the formal that'll show them, *cancel the formal!* Wendy cries *that'll teach them, punish them, show them about consequences.* Wendy from Geography red-faced ranting like one of the Year Nine girls she hates, ranting about them being nothing but animals, *they are all on their way to prison,* about how giving them anything but life lessons comes back to bite us.

Keeping it real held over till next week.

Meeting over—handsome student teacher smiles—follows me—runs his hands through his long dark hair holds out an iPod tells me he confiscated it and forgot to give it back… I'll take it, I say and he hands over the orange iPod, I have the iPod in my hand. I'll return it then shall I? I'll…

> PETCHALL *puts the earphones into her ears. She stops and listens to the iPod.*
>
> *A plane.*

♦ ♦ ♦

TAMARA: Fucking Tuesday again.

Laurence doesn't surface his door shut as tight as his mouth.

No note on the table saying have a good day saying have an okay day saying have any kind of fucking day at all.

Kitchen smells like garbage—fuck knows how since there's nothing to make garbage with.

Then he's awake in the doorway, grey as the clouds in the sky saying/

LAURENCE: What's all the racket?

TAMARA: Looking for something to eat.

He opens the fridge door.

No milk no juice no cereal no bread no butter no leftovers 'cause we had nothing last night.

Nothing inside but half a shrivelled lemon—like you.

LAURENCE: What?

TAMARA: That lemon. Like you. Neglect.

LAURENCE: What?

TAMARA: This is neglect. I want a fuckin' feed.

Fridge full of shit like.

I gotta go.

I don't look back at Laurence. Cragged-up old faggot. Hate him.
What chance he give me?

A bell.

♦ ♦ ♦

LEANNE *waits at the gate.*

TAMARA: She's there at the gate where Squid should be. Standing there
lipstick matching her bag enough to scare anyone away—sure Squid
saw her and ran—what does she want? Maybe Virgin found out what
she's like and sacked her—maybe she dumped her second chance
kids kept the money from Johan and went and filled up the Prius with
things for me to eat maybe shit doesn't come out your arse…

She stinks of something fake.

What do you want? She says/

LEANNE: Nice way to greet your mum.

I sent you two messages today, Tamara.

TAMARA: Which'll make up for what exactly? Didn't get 'em.

LEANNE: Give me a kiss.

TAMARA: Mum!

LEANNE: I need to tell you something.

TAMARA: What?

LEANNE: Shall we go to a coffee shop?

TAMARA: Round here? Where do you reckon we are?

LEANNE: There must be somewhere.

TAMARA: You bring that Dettol stuff you use on your hands before you
eat?

There's not and I can't/

LEANNE: Why?

TAMARA: Gotta be in class. School Certificate coming. Want me to fail?

LEANNE: Of course not, Tammy.

TAMARA: Don't call me that.

LEANNE: I just/

TAMARA: What do you want to tell me? You changed your mind and
suddenly care? What do you want to tell me?

LEANNE: I'd like to talk to you.

LEANNE/TAMARA: sms.

TAMARA: Phones in our hands and they both look the same—I have her hands. That's too much. I gotta...

They both look at their messages.

SQUID: in the park babe wassup? bring us a smoke

TAMARA: I gotta go—maybe talk on the weekend.

LEANNE: We won't be able to, Tamara. I should've said something to you before.

TAMARA: What?

LEANNE: We've all been so busy. No excuse really/

TAMARA: Next week.

LEANNE: But... Johan and the girls and I/

TAMARA: Dickhead and the spoilt brats. What about them?

LEANNE: We're moving.

TAMARA: Moving?

LEANNE: To Brisbane.

TAMARA: You're moving to Brisbane?

LEANNE: Yes.

TAMARA: Sorry?

LEANNE: I should've...

TAMARA: You fucking bet you should've.

LEANNE: You can fly up. For holidays or/

TAMARA: What?

LEANNE: I'll talk to your dad?

TAMARA: Holidays or what? Talk to Dad? How?

LEANNE: Tamara? Tam?

TAMARA: Leave me alone, you fucking cow.

LEANNE: Tamara.

TAMARA: Traffic moving quickly on the street if you walk fast and don't look back won't hear it—that shit she's been spitting out for years. Thinking of all her lies piled on each other—the first time I remember knowing she is lying seeing her face as she swears to Dad we'd been shopping when I been sitting in the car out the front of Johan's with a Diet Coke and a bag of Starburst to keep me quiet.

Put on iPod really fucking loud.

Music beating fast this track kills her that whining.

Bitch—want to smash something—bitch want this sound to blow that bitch.

> TAMARA *puts in her earphones. Stands there. It's clear she doesn't know what she should actually do. She walks.*

♦ ♦ ♦

DANE: They tried lots of things. To get me on track. Rick, this muscle guy with tatts'd come to school from a circus Mondays. We'd get taken out of class do handstands juggling cartwheels and shit. Used to all be there Monday for Rick. He was really fucking strong. He could lift me up onto his shoulders without even trying. And he took me aside and said I was good that if I could apply myself like I had in other ways I'd surprise myself. And 'cause I was coming to school again, they put me back on the team. Everything was ace.

> *He juggles.*

Rick said to me that if my mind could be as strong as my body I would do anything I wanted, teachers saying to me that if I didn't change the way I was doing things I'd end up… here.

When I get out of here… Things are gonna be different. Gonna put my mind to that.

Few things to get out of my system first. Things I been thinking about. Things I need to do. Give myself a week. Then…

♦ ♦ ♦

TAMARA *with a bundle of paper, then* PETCHALL.

PETCHALL: Voice outside the staffroom then:

TEACHER: Why are you up here during lunch?

TAMARA: Need to see Miss Petchall.

TEACHER: Helen, student here to see you.

TAMARA: Hi *Helen.*

PETCHALL: What's that?

TAMARA: My story. The one I was telling you about.

> You in shock, Miss?

PETCHALL: No. Pleased. Excited. Thrilled even.

TAMARA: Need to show you 'cause it's better than the other one.

> TAMARA *looks at* PETCHALL *with intensity. Nearly smiles but doesn't.*

You'll read it?

PETCHALL: Of course I will.

TAMARA: It's a love story, Miss.

PETCHALL: A love story! Thank you, Tamara, I could use something a bit steamy in my day.

TAMARA: Oh Miss!

PETCHALL: I'm looking forward to reading it, Tamara. You better go down to the quad now.

I'll walk with you. I've got duty. Did you have lunch?

TAMARA: I'm not anorexical.

> TAMARA *stares at a boy sitting by himself in the corridor.*

PETCHALL: Hello Raymond.

TAMARA: Ay, ya great fucking spaz. Answer her.

PETCHALL: Tamara! Raymond, are you/

TAMARA: I'm talking to ya, sped—speds like you shouldn't come here, shouldn't come here 'cause you take up so much time and we get nothing, normal kids like us get nothing.

PETCHALL: Tamara!

> TAMARA *smiles suddenly sweet.*

TAMARA: Nothing wrong with calling them sped, Miss, it's just special ed.

We learnt about it in English with you. Abbreviation Miss.

PETCHALL: But…

> *Lights go out, everything dark.* TAMARA *squeals with delight.*

Turn on the light!

> TAMARA *lets out a little cackle.*

Whoever did that, turn on the light. Right now.

TAMARA: You scared, Miss? Speds and teachers hate the dark.

> *We hear a tussle and the lights come on.* TAMARA *and* RAYMOND *have vanished.* PETCHALL *is alone.*

PETCHALL: Raymond? Tamara?

The bell rings longer than usual. It jolts PETCHALL.

The band rehearsal begins, they struggle to find a tune. All the things you hear in these corridors. Things teachers say to kids, things kids say to each other. And all those bells echo.

◆ ◆ ◆

SQUID *waits in the laneway for* TAMARA.

SQUID: Where you been?

TAMARA: Doesn't matter.

SQUID: You okay?

TAMARA: Don't ask me that. Serious, if you ask me that again.

SQUID: What?

TAMARA: If I'm fucking okay.

SQUID: Sorry.

TAMARA: And don't say fucking sorry. Why do you ask me that?

SQUID: Want to know.

You talk a lot but I never really know—

TAMARA: You want one of those relationships. What gave you that idea?

Hate talking that shit—fucking feelings.

SQUID: What's up?

TAMARA: Fucking Bloomfield had a go at me in Hospitality—*you can't do prac in those shoes.*

That bitch. Why can't I wear open-toe shoes if you are?

I'm a teacher—yeah but your ugly old feet'll burn the same as mine if I drop a saucepan of hot shit on them, fucking dog. Sent me to Dietz.

SQUID: Why?

TAMARA: *Language. Bad language at school means trouble at home.*

Like derr. Dietz is a lame-fuck counsellor anyhow, she just fiddles with her fingernails.

Pause.

Six weeks today.

SQUID: Yeah? Happy six weeks.

TAMARA: You stink. Why you all sweaty?

SQUID: Smith let us play tackle in PE. I got away with royal blue shorts.

TAMARA: You miss it, don't you?

You could go back and play.

You should.

SQUID: Can't. When my brother went to court things came out.

TAMARA: What do you mean?

SQUID: They said he'd been selling shit at the club.

TAMARA: But that wasn't you.

SQUID: No. But he was their best player. Like some god. And then…

TAMARA: Play for another club.

SQUID: You kidding? That'd be worse than dealing drugs.

    Pause.

TAMARA: Saw the CD cover you made in Art. Mad.

SQUID: Desilva kept saying it was fully trippy.

TAMARA: She said mine's *superficial.* What would she know?

That assignment sucked—no-one buys CDs anymore. But yours is real mad. You with eight arms and a forked tongue and all those muscles. Desilva held it up in our class and showed it off. She had a full-on wet spot after. She stared at it for ages, you looking like some sea god.

SQUID: A squid god.

TAMARA: All those muscles. Yeah, right.

SQUID: Gonna get it tattooed.

TAMARA: What?

SQUID: A squid.

TAMARA: Yeah? Where?

Can't get a tattoo till you're eighteen.

SQUID: Not waiting.

TAMARA: Everyone has to wait.

SQUID: Nobody has to wait if they don't want to.

TAMARA: They do.

You missed assembly.

Rowney went on about the fight. That chink kid Thahn's in intensive care. Heaps of girls crying after.

SQUID: 'Cause he's in hospital?

TAMARA: Na. They threatened to cancel the formal.

SQUID: Why?

TAMARA: 'Cause we're animals.

SQUID: They won't.

TAMARA: Na, just a threat.

Stupid bitches, all they care about's the formal.

They cheered when he was getting bashed, then loaded it onto YouTube.

SQUID: Never follow through with threats.

TAMARA: Na.

SQUID: Gonna get the tattoo for the formal. Lift up me shirt on the dance floor and…

TAMARA: Buy the tickets first then get the tattoo.

SQUID: So. You coming with me?

TAMARA: Suppose.

SQUID: Cool.

TAMARA: Don't get my name on you.

SQUID: As if.

TAMARA: Why wouldn't ya?

SQUID: Just wouldn't.

TAMARA: Good. It's trashy. My dad's got Leanne tattooed on his arm.

SQUID: What's wrong with that?

TAMARA: My mum's a total bitch. And Dad's a fag now.

SQUID: Your dad's a faggot?

TAMARA: Yep. A fag with *Leanne* tattooed on his arm.

SQUID: He wasn't always a fag, then?

TAMARA *looks at* SQUID *incredulously.*

TAMARA: Go home, Jase.

SQUID: Kiss me.

TAMARA: Na—you reek.

They kiss. SQUID *smiles at her, leaves.* TAMARA *remains.*

DANE *is released from prison.*

DANE: Aunty stands there in her best dress clutching her bag to her chest—waiting watching the traffic passing the prison.

DANE/AUNTY: I'm out./ You're out.

DANE: Look she gives me worse than any look I got inside—she sighs like it hurts to breathe—takes out an envelope—hands it to me.

Don't need money, Aunty./ Take it. Take it./

AUNTY: Take it./ Take it./

DANE: She says. Don't want it./

AUNTY: Take it.

Where you gonna go, Dane? Don't want you back. You can get your stuff but you can't come back./ Lock's changed. Don't try anything.

DANE: Lock's changed. Don't try anything.

    AUNTY *and* DANE *go separate ways.*

TAMARA: Get home

slam the door

sit on my bed

stare out window at the weeds, the dirt where the herbs grew—the rusted barbeque.

Cover my face in a pillow suffocate myself feel what it's like—the light at the top.

Dizzy.

Stop. Just before I…

Send Dezzie a message—

nothing back

smoke out the window

nothing back

update my status—no-one on Facebook.

Pissed off.

Everyone hassling you when you don't need it and then—when you want them—want to tell them something…

Check phone check Facebook nothing.

Nothing back.

Just want them to know I'm going to the…

Think about the formal. Me coming downstairs in my dress—Dad's mouth dropping. Dad smiling at me like he used to smile at… her.

Used to sit on their bed and watch Mum put on perfume for him.

She'd spray it and walk right through the mist like a film star.

Dad'd smell it and smile—kiss the back of her neck.

Six weeks three days four hours—me and Squid.

He'll look hot in a tux. We'll turn up together in a white stretch limo him like a football god and me like a rock star. My killer dress and my killer hair.

The moment we walk in together.

Cameras flashing and us dancing together in the middle of the dance floor right under the mirror ball.

Something to look forward to.

END OF ACT ONE

ACT TWO

The lockdown bell rings.

PETCHALL: So many questions. Questions people would have asked over and over again. What happened that day? Did I sense that the boy, because they always call them that, did I sense the boy was…? Was he on edge? Was he taking something? Had he been taking something?

In classes the week leading up to the incident how had his behaviour been? Did he sit up the back and stare out a window or did he fidget like pins had been stuck in all over his legs and arms or did he do work? If he did work, what work was done? Did anything he did or wrote or said signify anything? So many questions.

What were his family like? Did he have friends? How did he relate to the other kids in the class? Was he a leader or a follower?

And then of the day. Questions about the time it happened, about the weather about what I was teaching when the lockdown bell rang and did I think it was a drill because schools have drills and what made me realise that it wasn't a drill—that it was actually happening?

◆ ◆ ◆

SQUID *enters, then* TAMARA.

TAMARA: Excursion Wednesday. Careers expo in the city sitting up the back/ of the bus.

TEACHER: We are letting you all go today but do not abuse the trust. Be mindful of your behaviour/ that you are in public,

TAMARA/SQUID: Yeah yeah.

TAMARA: Careers expo, heaps of stalls giving away showbags full of logo-covered shit—crap bribes to make you want to be a nurse or a teacher or…

Free food 'n' shit—Subway's here, look/

SQUID: Yeah, that chick's a babe.

TAMARA: She's a lying slut in a Subway uniform—look at the way she's smiling at him as if you'd have a career there shithouse pay—fooling

all them fat people—smell of that bread in your hair every day till…
I'll go and tell her my boyfriend works there and he can't even afford
to buy me/ [formal tickets.]

SQUID: Don't.

TAMARA: Bloke from the army looks you in the eye—reckons he's
summed us both up tells you not to worry too much about study just
as long as you finish.

Bloke from the army gives you a go of a gun asks me if I reckon you'd
look good in the uniform, better than him but he's like seventy-five.

Looks at you whispers *you ever wanted to drive a tank?*

You ever want to get shot in the guts maybe get your head blown
off?

He wants to drive a Nissan Skyline not a tank. He told me. You don't
want to kill shit do you?

SQUID: Shut up. Just talking/

TAMARA: He seen us both coming/

SQUID: Just/

TAMARA: Rather work for Subway than that/

SQUID: Not so bad.

TAMARA: Yeah. Whatever. They marked the roll already. Let's get out of
here, go into the city.

SQUID: Want to look around a bit.

TAMARA: At what?

SQUID: Dunno.

TAMARA: Don't get you. What's the point?

Kids everywhere carrying showbags wearing new caps some full-
on dogs from a private school stare at me and whisper something.
Fucking stuck-up cows.

I look around and someone else is trying to con you. Honest Jasyn,
you don't get it.

Fuck it. You don't want to come. I'm going. Gonna fuck this propa-
ganda fest off.

TAMARA *puts on her iPod and goes.*

SQUID *puts on a cap with a logo on it looks around to show* TAMARA,
realises she has gone.

PETCHALL: In my handbag—the confiscated iPod.

> *She takes out the iPod and, as covertly as her students, listens to it.*

I turn it up—full bore in the careers show Eminem some gangsta rap—*smack up the boy in the baseball cap*. A space between me and the expo—and everybody moving in time. It's like some drug that keeps things out insulates me from the drone of it all and I feel incredible. Invincible.

SQUID: sms

wherd you go?

> *Pause.*

No answer, nothing.

PETCHALL: Near the navy stand I see this boy with ice-blue eyes. He stares at me, look on his face like… Reminds me of Lucas Milakovski—quiet boy who just arrived at the back of my class one day. He never smiled once. Always stunk of smoke. Lucas died. I read it in the paper. Dead before he was twenty-one. High on something, tried to do a runner from a taxi went the wrong way got hit by a truck. Boys you never see again just hear about. Russell Lyndam, Manfred Jacob, Jay Keane, Malcolm Sheenan, Daryl Tapp, Peter Galea, Ahmet Kozkus.

> *She turns off the iPod, puts it back in her purse. Goes.*

SQUID: You aren't on the bus back to school.

You aren't with the other girls.

No sms nothing.

Go to work thinking maybe you'll drop by.

At work. Make your favourite sub. Ready in case you come by. With extra cheese in case you…

> SQUID *goes.*

◆ ◆ ◆

We hear a fight, windows smashing, things being thrown, screaming, then sirens.

TAMARA: Leanne comes over stands at the door tells Laurence she's leaving and that's the end of taking me on the weekends and the end of the money.

He goes apeshit—lashes out—goes mental.

Breaks things says things breaks things windows and shit throws stuff slams up Johan's car he's just sitting in it waiting for her to drop her bombs.

Windscreen smashes glass showers all over everything.

Front door off its hinges.

People up the street come down—stare at it all happening.

Me saying frig off don't need youse all lookin'.

Mum screaming one minute sobbing the next. Sirens.

Josie from two doors up putting her arm round me pulling me into her sitting room making tea saying I should stay inside for a while till it settles down but I can hear everything anyway the smashing and Dad yelling and Johan shouting and Mum screaming all of them at once and then nothing but sirens. Police come.

They can tell what happened all they see is broken glass and blood on the wall in the hall on Mum's white dress.

Police take Dad away.

What if they lock him up? It wasn't his fault that's all and when I was… I don't want them to take me 'cause…

This is shit. Will they take me? This has happened before and they took me.

Not his fault. He needs me. Dad, he…

Quiet in the street now. Jerry on his porch looks the other way—front door hanging. Don't shut properly. Won't lock.

Silent inside the house. Nothing. Dad's string thing broken with everything else.

Don't know where Dad is.

He needs me. Dad needs me. But when I ask where he is if he's still at the cops—

no-one says nothing.

> TAMARA *listens to her iPod.*

> SQUID, *elsewhere does the same. He goes.*

Dad messages me… he's at the hospital.

I go to see him. Maybe bring him home.

He looks pale, sick. I say you going to be alright Dad? 'Cause I do. I do. I do. Love him. He's sick. He looks really… but he tells me these are just cuts and bruises from…

The bell rings.

Nurse says she wants to talk to me about Dad.

I don't want to hear it but she says it anyway and I'm thinking how long is it Dad—how long is it that he has known that he has had it and she says—nobody knows how long he's had it but he just found out as well. Ten things in my head crash hard red glass smashes everywhere, ice, blood everywhere. She says your dad has HIV. Dad's got AIDS.

How will I remember this? With smashing glass from the windscreen and the kids up the street laughing at all of us? The dumb song they are singing on some kids' show on afternoon TV just as they tell me that my dad…

A plane.

Nurse says is there anything you'd like to ask like to know I say I need a smoke. Blood pounding in my head walk out onto the street. How did he get it? Who gave it to him was it their fault or his—why did he get it? Will I get it?—What if he uses my toothbrush or spits on my plate or infects the toilet—have I got it? How can you be sure I haven't got it already? Will he die? If he dies what'll happen to me, who should I tell who shouldn't I tell?

She smokes. DANE *approaches.*

Get out of the hospital, to think—smoke try to call you Squid but your phone's off and that's where I run into him. He's watching me smoking and I feel him looking at me something from his eyes some energy and he smiles looks at me comes over and says/

DANE: You got a smoke?

TAMARA: Yeah.

DANE: Gave up but/

TAMARA: What?

DANE: Feel like one.

TAMARA: They aren't cheap, ya know.

DANE: You want some money for one?

TAMARA: Na. Here you go.

She gives him one.

He's a man—not a boy—grins at me like he knows what I'm thinking. Tattoos on his arm and wrist everywhere his chest back of his neck. How many tattoos you got?

DANE: Twenty-three.

TAMARA: I can only see six.

Muscley too. What you do?

DANE: Play footy, work out and shit.

TAMARA: He smells like beer, smells like a man.

DANE: I'm Dane.

SQUID: Think about you all day—don't hear from you.

TAMARA: Tamara.

DANE: G'day Tamara.

SQUID: Don't hear from you. Out of credit?

TAMARA: He doesn't say call you Tammy or Tam or nothing. Just/

DANE: You look upset.

TAMARA: Kind of. Shit day.

DANE: That's why you look sad.

SQUID: Call you but. Call all day.

TAMARA: How would you know? You seen me before?

And when he smiles like that it hits me.

They look at each other for some time.

DANE: You sure have grown up.

TAMARA: And I'm about to say all sorts of shit. I'm about to say all sorts of shit but I don't. I don't. Nor does he.

DANE *winks, leaves.*

He gets my mobile number says he'll use it but he has a few things to take care of.

Old man in pyjamas with a drip in his arm stares at me as I watch Dane go. What? What?

Nurse comes out calls me back in. Says I should go and see Dad.

I turn around to see if Dane's gone. He looks back at the same time winks turns a corner.

Dad's lying in bed watching TV some shitty infomercial endless talk sipping something from a plastic cup.

Stares at me. Asks: How much do you know?

> TAMARA *puts her earphones on. She says nothing. Just stares out.*

SQUID: Exam tomorrow—you wrote the date in my diary—put a love heart in the 'a'—who loves tests? We're meant to study tonight. It was your idea. You said you'd cook some tea and we'd go through all the shit we need to. And I got a surprise for you too. Can't wait to see you face.

> *A bell rings.*

But I don't.

PETCHALL: In my hand a piece of paper with one name on it. Tamara Brewster absent from the exam. Not like her.

Headmaster's on the phone in his office some parent ranting you can tell by the plummy voice and the way he's saying *yes yes yes yes yes yes clearly we'll do what we can.*

Then I see her walking up the corridor.

Tamara?

Standing there shaking, trying to catch your breath that's fast like you've been running.

You alright?

TAMARA: Didn't get much sleep.

PETCHALL: Breathing quick, glaring at that painting of a sleeping cat on the wall outside the office.

TAMARA: Tried to get here fast. Ran. When I went to the hall they wouldn't let me go in.

PETCHALL: Stretching the hole in the sleeve of your jumper.

TAMARA: Got to do the exam, Miss. If I don't… Need to see Rowney— push open the door—can't wait—push open the door.

PETCHALL: I'm behind you as you stare at Rowney—he looks up says *I'm going to have to call you back* puts down the phone is about to tell you what you shouldn't do that you shouldn't just come in like that that doors are meant for knocking on/ but

TAMARA: But I'm missing the exam.

PETCHALL: He looks at me then you, at/ what you're wearing.

TAMARA: What I'm wearing. I got to do it, Sir. If I don't do that exam…

PETCHALL: He takes a deep breath and stands reaches out to touch you I'm sure it's a touch but it looks like a push. *Just give us a moment Tamara please.* He says *she's too late and she can't go in wearing that. Can you deal with her* he whispers, picks up the phone and pushes the door close to shut just a little slit a cat's eye looking through.

TAMARA: I need to be in the hall now, Miss.

PETCHALL: What's happened, Tamara?

TAMARA: Nothing.

PETCHALL: Nothing?

TAMARA: Stuff at home.

PETCHALL: What stuff?

TAMARA: Don't want to talk about it. Shit happened. I need to do the exam, Miss.

PETCHALL: I know that, Tamara, but there are regulations.

TAMARA: Regulations?

PETCHALL: Mr Rowney won't let you do the exam/ because you're not in uniform.

TAMARA: Because I'm not in uniform? You got to be fucking kidding me, Miss.

PETCHALL: I'll look in lost property—see what I can do. Wait here.

> PETCHALL *goes.* TAMARA *sits. Plays with her phone. She receives an sms.*

TAMARA: sms

DANE: hey babe, wot u doing got wheels u wanna go for a drive?

> sms

TAMARA: wot like right now?

> sms

DANE: like when else?

> TAMARA *weighs things up, then smiles to herself as she leaves.*

> PETCHALL *returns with a uniform, too late.*

SQUID: Empty seat up the front in the exam—weird you not being here. Don't hear nothing from you after and I got such a great surprise for you too—can't wait. I got the formal tickets—just like you asked—just like/

TAMARA: Eight weeks four days seven hours. I'll say I didn't know. I'll say I didn't realise. That it was your brother 'cause I thought he was in jail. Doesn't feel like cheating when we meet at the park.

Him sitting in this ute opening the door for me.

DANE: Hey.

TAMARA: Hey.

They kiss.

Doesn't feel like cheating till we stop on the road by the sea, Dane's arms—his smile and him knowing what to do. Doesn't feel like cheating till you ring me.

Her phone rings.

DANE: Who's that?

TAMARA: No-one.

When you aren't ringing me you cross my mind once. I imagine you putting ham on stinking bread and standing outside Subway smoking—looking to see if I'm coming up the street with a Red Bull for your break. But I'm not. I'm with Dane. Dane and me we get Chinese he eats it—hate batter.

DANE: I'm staying in Coogee real close to the water.

TAMARA: I shouldn't/

DANE: You like skinny dipping?

TAMARA: Dane and I drive for a bit past all these big houses then we stop at the flat he shows me garden the bedroom the view of the water. You call again. Your name on the screen. Press reject. Switch you off.

A bell rings.

Don't sleep—not a bit. Dane and I up all night. Nothing else in my head either—not you Squid not Laurence and I don't need to say nothing to Dane about anything if it's not in my head.

He kisses me—morning sun peeking through like a spy through the slit in the blind.

DANE: You need to get to work or anything?

TAMARA: Yeah.

DANE: So you work now? Not at school?

TAMARA: Yeah. Na. School.

DANE: How old are you now?

TAMARA: Told ya last night.

Where you heading?

DANE: Visit my aunty.

TAMARA: Drop me off near there?

Sitting next to Dane in the traffic—the radio makes it sound like it's the best morning ever—the jokes—the song they're playing when we stop at the corner of your street Squid. Can just see your house.

DANE: Let you out here.

They kiss. TAMARA *lingers longer than* DANE.

TAMARA: For a second I get shit scared you might see—but you don't. Too early. No-one sees. Go to 7-Eleven, three Diet Red Bull and a donut. Kids from school, uniforms everywhere, it all comes back, the exam how I've fucked things up. I've fucked things up.

DANE: Aunty opening the door before I can test the old key saying,

AUNTY: Your brother's inside having breakfast—go and say hello.

DANE: Hey bro. You're up early… sweet dreams?

SQUID: Dane. You're out.

DANE: Looks like it.

They look at each other, don't quite know what to do.

SQUID: Sick tatt, man. That new?

DANE: A few new ones.

SQUID: Show us.

He does.

SQUID/DANE: Aunty tutting.

DANE: It's my body, Aunty.

Didn't she tell ya I was coming out?

SQUID: Didn't say when. Didn't expect… but it's sick. We can…

DANE: What?

SQUID: Dunno.

You staying? Where's ya stuff?

DANE: Stuff?

    Can't stay.

SQUID: Not staying here?

DANE: Just pick up some things.

SQUID: What you gonna do?

DANE: What do ya mean?

SQUID: What you gonna do?

DANE: You sound like her. I'll sort it out. What the fuck's the problem?

    Pause.

SQUID: Dane.

DANE: What Jasyn?

SQUID: Sorry.

DANE: Sorry? What for?

SQUID: Not much of a brother. Didn't come to visit much.

DANE: Yeah?

SQUID: Yeah.

    I better to go to school.

    A plane.

PETCHALL: Open them up then and if you haven't brought them you were asked to, so no fussing. Hope you have a late note, Tamara.

TAMARA: They're reading, Ezie stammers as he reads out loud—*The Outsiders* greasers and socs—something a sped could read a book for speds words like pus dripping slowly from a rotten cut.

PETCHALL: Sit down, Tamara, everyone listening/

TAMARA: Squid in class before me for the first time ever mouths:/ Where you been?

SQUID: Where you been?

    Where you been?

TAMARA: Knock on the door.

    Dumb little messenger with a bowl cut holds a pink release note get-out-of-jail card.

PETCHALL: Tamara.

TAMARA: Yes Miss?

PETCHALL: You need to see Mr Rowney after the lesson. About the exam.

TAMARA: Yes Miss. Squid still staring at me, raises his eyebrow.

A bell rings.

SQUID: Where you been?

TAMARA: Tell you later. Gotta see Rowney.

SQUID: Tell me now/

TAMARA: Leave me alone.

Wait outside the office door.

PETCHALL: No barging in today./

TAMARA: No tears no drama not today and I'm in my uniform.

PETCHALL: She's in no hurry. She'd be happy to wait for the rest of the day in front of the cat in the picture on the wall/

TAMARA: Smell of pies from the canteen drifting down the hall shut my eyes/

PETCHALL: Tamara.

TAMARA: Following me, Miss?

PETCHALL: You look tired.

TAMARA: A bit.

PETCHALL: Not sleeping well?

TAMARA: You could say that.

PETCHALL: Did you/

TAMARA: I had breakfast.

PETCHALL: Good.

What happened to you yesterday?

You disappeared. I think you should have a talk with Miss Dietz?

TAMARA: No-one speaks with her, kids run rings around her make-up stories, fake shit.

PETCHALL: That's not very kind.

TAMARA: So?

PETCHALL: Miss Dietz might be able to help.

TAMARA: She stinks of smokes.

PETCHALL: So do you.

Miss Dietz can help you if you go and see her.

TAMARA: Rather speak to you.

PETCHALL: Your mum came up to the school this morning.

TAMARA: Ha.

PETCHALL: She's worried about you.

TAMARA: Yeah right.

Worried I'll turn out like her?

PETCHALL: She called—said you haven't been home.

TAMARA: How would she know?

PETCHALL: She's come to look after you while your father is in hospital.
Where did you sleep? Tamara, where did you stay?

TAMARA: Kids in other places in the school write shit add shit bake shit
burn shit—

Not saying nothing.

PETCHALL: Tamara?

TAMARA: Not going to tell you if you're going to tell her.

PETCHALL: I just need to know/

TAMARA: What?

PETCHALL: Where you're staying.

Tamara?

TAMARA: With a friend.

PETCHALL: You're only fifteen, Tamara.

TAMARA: So? Don't need this right now.

PETCHALL: I'm sorry?

TAMARA: You heard me.

PETCHALL: We just need to know you're safe.

Is it with Jasyn? Are you staying with him?

TAMARA: As if I'd stay there.

PETCHALL: Where then? The school has a legal/ obligations.

TAMARA: Just leave me alone. I'm fine.

PETCHALL: Tamara.

TAMARA: I don't have to say.

PETCHALL: I'm going to get you to have a talk with Miss Dietz.

TAMARA: Out in the carpark where all the teachers smoke?

PETCHALL: It doesn't matter where it happens, we just need to know that
you're safe. Your mum wants you to come home now.

TAMARA: Home?

PETCHALL: Yes.

TAMARA: My *mum* wants me to come *home*? Doesn't that sound nice?

PETCHALL: That's what she said, Tamara.

TAMARA: Did you ask her to define home? The one she left or the new one she has that she keeps me out of like I'm some dog.

PETCHALL: No. I know you've having a rough time.

It can't be easy.

TAMARA: What can't?

PETCHALL: Things with your dad. With the… news.

TAMARA: What do you know about that?

What is it with schools? You find out everything.

PETCHALL: It's so we can try and help.

TAMARA: Help? How can you help? Check I'm in uniform?

PETCHALL: What would you like us to do?

TAMARA: Everything's gone bad and it's closing in around me. Do something. Stop it. Click your fingers or something and make it stop. Give me something better?

PETCHALL: I can't/

TAMARA: Of course you can't. Teachers can't do shit.

Not staying here anyway. Why bother?

PETCHALL: What are you talking about, Tamara?

TAMARA: I'm leaving.

What's the point? You try to do things right and they fuck up anyway. I hate everything about this place. Everyone knows your fucking business and it's all so friggin'/ boring.

PETCHALL: You're upset.

TAMARA: Yeah.

PETCHALL: But you're a good student. You have a good future.

TAMARA: You reckon?

PETCHALL: We just need to know you are safe. Need to know if we can help support you/

TAMARA: Or what?

PETCHALL: Or what nothing, Tamara.

Let's talk later when you've had a chance to settle down.

I'll give you a note to go back to class.

TAMARA: I'm not going back to sit in that shit box. You can keep your notes and all your concern for some other case.

    She goes.

PETCHALL: Follow but I'm too slow. Ladies in the office point to the swinging doors.

♦ ♦ ♦

TAMARA: sms

SQUID: u still in there?

    sms

TAMARA: no.

    sms

SQUID: where r u?

    sms

TAMARA: fuck you fuck off

    sms

SQUID: nice. u in the park?

    sms

TAMARA: no

    sms

SQUID: u ok?

    sms.

    Nothing.

TAMARA: Stand on street get on the bus. Sit on the back seat looking down at people in cars in traffic women on phones in four-wheel drives and men in fluoro uniforms driving utes. Think about Dane and his arms and his smile and how he said the way you do that you sure wouldn't know you were only seventeen. Seventeen.

Make plans for me and Dane. I could learn to surf—he'd like that—reckon he'll let me live at his place for a while till I found a job till I got on my feet a bit...

Get off in the city near the posh arcade. Stand in the shadows of buildings people in suits huddled smoking—group of private school girls in hats and ties walking in a line—follow them nothing else to do.

Follow them along the street past Town Hall teacher saying to a girl up the front even if you're thirsty don't drink in public wait until we get there and you can drink *ladies don't drink in the street.*

Cross the park, past the cathedral hear the wind whistling up the street. Traffic charging past.

Watch three girls hang back and wait.

Watch them turn around and laugh—rip off their hats and ties and jackets shove them in their bags and walk the other way—hear them talking about their formal just like those cashed-up bitches in my year and they stop and look into a shop with blank-faced mannequins in the window wearing these dresses.

Awesome dresses. My dress—silver like spoons and mirrors and clouds full of raindrops—the dress I always imagined. One of the mannequins wearing my dress. She knows it—looks embarrassed. Caught you!

Two of the girls go up the steps into the shop. The other one stays on the street.

We look at each other.

She looks at me like she knows everything about me my dad my mum—my broken front door how much money I got in my pocket. Then she looks the other way—there's this handsome guy coming towards me—he waves and I think he's waving at me but then—he walks straight past me—kisses her and they walk into the shop laughing together.

She puts on her iPod.

Sit on the street outside Gloria Jean's. Make an iced mocha last the afternoon. Thinking what am I doing? What have I done?

Walk home. Brace myself for Mum but find Dad back from hospital asleep on the stained couch in front of the blaring tele in the living room all these pills in bottles laid out on the coffee table. And I'm not thinking of Dane anymore I'm thinking about you Squid. Remembering the way that girl and her boyfriend looked at each other before they kissed and how they laughed as they went up the stairs together to choose a dress for that girl to wear to their formal.

◆ ◆ ◆

PETCHALL: I see a face from some class years back. She's pretty—she's in a uniform sitting behind the steering wheel of an ambulance. *Hey Miss* she says and smiles. Hello Mei Ling. *Do you remember me* she asks? Yes. *Do you remember us all?* No. I remember the ones I thought might be forgotten if I didn't.

My desk covered in essays, trousers with ink stains pockets full of ink and the echoes. Years ago what my mother said about becoming a school teacher. Telling me that school teachers never grow up because they never leave school so they never get a chance to go out into the real world.

◆ ◆ ◆

TAMARA *goes to visit* SQUID.

TAMARA: Sunday morning—knock on your door stand there wondering what the fuck I'm gonna say to you—the truth all around me. Your aunty answers—tells me where you are—inside's clean—smells like eucalyptus—Squid?

Wake you up?

SQUID: Yeah, but I'm glad. Where you been?

TAMARA: Around. You get my texts?

Why didn't you answer?

SQUID: Why didn't you answer? Last few days I been calling you. Wish you'd answered then 'cause I needed to talk.

Where were you?

TAMARA: Doesn't matter. Shit happening, that's all.

SQUID: Shit happening for me too.

You okay?

TAMARA: No. You?

SQUID: No.

A plane.

Wanna come up to my room?

TAMARA: Alright.

SQUID: Aunty—better keep the door open.

TAMARA: Where's all your stuff?

SQUID: What stuff?

TAMARA: Look out the window—I can see the corner where I got out of Dane's ute. While you were asleep in that bed under that orange blanket…

SQUID: I got something for you. For us./ Formal tickets.

TAMARA: Formal tickets.

    Silence.

SQUID: You happy?

TAMARA: Yeah. You?

SQUID: Yeah.

TAMARA: There's a fair in the park—wanna go?

♦ ♦ ♦

At the fair day in the park. We hear music.

TAMARA: Tents in the park.

    Stalls and rides and/

SQUID: Look.

TAMARA: An octopus, arms reaching up to the sky—bright green octopus head in the middle with a big grin like it's…

SQUID: Happy.

TAMARA: Like it's off its head.

    Shakira crackles in the speakers.

    Carnie guy nods at us—toothpick in his mouth.

SQUID: Want a ride?

    Be fun.

TAMARA: Na.

SQUID: Why?

TAMARA: All the fake screams, it couldn't be that scary.

SQUID: Na, it's going too slow.

TAMARA: Five bucks.

SQUID: Waste of money.

TAMARA: Yeah. Next to that, clowns' heads turn—mouths open wide and behind—the ugliest prizes I ever saw.

SQUID: I could win one for you.

TAMARA: Yeah right. Wouldn't be seen dead carrying that ugly shit around.

You reach out and grab my hand. Hold it tight—we walk together.

SQUID: I like this.

TAMARA: What?

SQUID: Having you next to me.

TAMARA: A big tent with a shiny floor, mirror ball spinning shooting flecks of sunlight, flecks float everywhere

a carnie in black stands there grinning at everything and nothing grinning like he had his brain nicked doesn't know what's going on—flecks of silver light on him his yellow teeth in all the mirrors.

SQUID: What is it?

TAMARA: Dunno.

They read the sign.

SQUID/TAMARA: Silent disco.

SQUID: What's that?

TAMARA: Why you always reckon I know shit?

SQUID: You do.

TAMARA: Silent disco. Full of people wearing earphones dancing.

SQUID: Look at them.

TAMARA: Swinging their arms,

bouncing,

stepping,

smiling.

But not a sound.

SQUID/TAMARA: Silent.

TAMARA: Just like the sign says.

SQUID: Pretty fucking sick.

TAMARA: Everyone with earphones looking in different directions— dancing but no music.

SQUID: You got your iPod?

TAMARA: Yeah.

SQUID: Want to dance?

Pick a tune for me. I'll pick one for you. We can swap.

TAMARA: You're meant to pay.

SQUID: Fuck that, that's for their music. We got our own.

TAMARA: Carnie taking tickets doesn't see us pass.

They swap earphones and dance.

I look around and see everyone in their own little world smiling— everyone dancing to their own tune not giving a fuck what anyone else has playing in their ears.

For one whole song everything like that.

You and me dance just like everyone else,

no-one tells us we shouldn't be there,

no-one tells us we are dancing the wrong steps or we don't know shit.

The Carnie winks at me and I look back at you Squid.

We face each other in the silent disco.

I look at your eyes—your tough eyes aren't tough aren't hard they're smiling. Right there and then—everything else blown away—just you and me Squid.

You so close I feel you breathe. We've never danced like this before. You reach out and pull me closer to you. The way you pull me in— makes me feel like I'm the best thing in the world.

They dance together. SQUID *stops.*

SQUID: I'm hungry. Want a hot dog?

TAMARA: From here? Na. Carnies cook them in their piss.

SQUID: Yeah?

TAMARA: Yeah.

SQUID: Gonna get one anyway.

TAMARA: Come straight back.

SQUID: I will.

SQUID *smiles at her and leaves.*

TAMARA *dances.*

DANE *enters the silent disco. He creeps up behind* TAMARA, *covers her eyes and gives her a long kiss. She doesn't realise it is him at first and pushes him off, then realises, pulls him back.* SQUID, *with hot dog, returns and witnesses this moment. He drops it on the grass and he runs.*

TAMARA: Jasyn! Squid.

> *She pushes* DANE *off.*

Time slows, time swings time dies and dangles from a treetop.

You run away and I'm there in the silent disco.

People around me dance and smile.

A couple fill the space we took as I watch you disappear.

> TAMARA *leaves.*

DANE: Easy to get stuff if you know where.

Shouldn't have told you that but I did.

Knew that when I said it—the way you looked at me.

And that's where you'll be I reckon.

Reckon I could find you, know the spot where you'll be.

Might go see if I'm right. But I know. It's in your blood.

Something above reaches down and pushes you into the night—just like it reached for me, pushed me into the night, Jasyn.

SQUID/DANE: The Cross.

SQUID: The fountain hissing,

DANE: Jap snapper tourists,

SQUID: Gangs in hoods—police vans,

DANE: Guys hot for their bit of the night./ Find stuff there fast.

SQUID: Find stuff there fast.

DANE: That's what I told you./ Stand in the laneway just up from Macca's

SQUID: Stand in the laneway just up from Macca's, right look on your face/ and you find it.

DANE: and you find it./ Easy.

SQUID: Easy.

DANE: Find it and BANG nothing matters/

SQUID: Find it and BANG nothing hurts/

DANE: Find it and/

SQUID/DANE: BANG nothing touches you nothing....

> *We see* SQUID *high on crystal meth.*
>
> *A bell rings a little longer than usual.*

TAMARA: Try and ring you Squid but your phone's off all the time that

Vodafone slut with her fucking obvious message tells me that over and over where are you?

PETCHALL: Questions you get asked/

TAMARA: Where have you been?

PETCHALL: Questions you ask yourself/

TAMARA: I'm sorry—you okay Squid?

PETCHALL: Questions nobody wants to ask/

TAMARA: Always a fucking/ Tuesday. Starts like any other.

PETCHALL: Tuesday. Starts like any other.

Get out of bed think today's the day I start walking to work—I walk. Listen to the iPod. Brisk/ walk resolve to give it back, get my own one in the Christmas sales.

TAMARA: Walk up our lane see our tags on the old bag's fence then…

> TAMARA *spots* PETCHALL *who is in her own world listening to her iPod and whistling.*

Miss.

Miss!

> TAMARA *taps her on the shoulder, scares her.*

What you listening to, Miss?

PETCHALL: Tamara. You scared the life out/

TAMARA: What is it?

> TAMARA *snatches the iPod and looks at the screen. Raises her eyebrows.*

No-one whistles anymore, Miss.

PETCHALL: Was I/

TAMARA: And teachers don't walk in laneways. You gotta be careful. There's a woman here that gets a look in her eyes meaner than any teacher.

PETCHALL: I read your love story.

TAMARA: Yeah?

PETCHALL: The bit at the end.

TAMARA: Yeah, crappy, ay?

PETCHALL: It's not. It's beautiful. It all works out, but not like you expect/

TAMARA: But it doesn't happen like that. Not really. Doesn't.

TAMARA/PETCHALL: Period one.

TAMARA: Miss again—more of Miss—more *Outsiders*—haircut gangs— no sign of you Squid then Miss says/

PETCHALL: Pens down, I'd like to stop a bit early.

TAMARA: Class groans Miss rolls her eyes—looks at me.

PETCHALL: I'd like to ask Tamara if she'd like to read something. If she could share something she's written with us all if/

TAMARA: Miss? What are you doing?

PETCHALL: I thought…

TAMARA: Not reading that to these speds not/

PETCHALL: And outside. It's started. In the laneway/

TAMARA: Squid painting shit about me on the walls.

PETCHALL: Ladies in the front office see him through the window—tell him to stop—to get off move to class/

TAMARA: But then they see his face. Mouths drop at once at the look in his eyes/

PETCHALL: They ring the Deputy the police the drug team the/

TAMARA: Me sitting there not knowing what's coming/

PETCHALL: Her sitting there saying/

TAMARA: Not reading that aloud, wish I'd never brung it in.

SQUID: World has split has broken has torn.

PETCHALL: Anger in his eyes.

TAMARA: How could you do that, Miss so—you are so insensitive.

PETCHALL: Anger in his eyes.

SQUID: Don't care who sees.

PETCHALL: Office ladies see Squid they call Rowney, the police.

TAMARA: Can't believe you did that, Miss.

SQUID: Out of it.

DANE: High as a fucking kite

PETCHALL: Out there./ We know nothing here.

TAMARA: We know nothing here.

DANE: High as a kite and he'll do it/ no-one'll stop him.

SQUID: No-one'll stop me.

I'm coming

Down the hallway spray red paint as I go.

TAMARA: On walls/

PETCHALL: On windows/

TAMARA: On lockers on/

SQUID: *Get out of my fucking way!*

> *Lockdown bell rings.*

PETCHALL: This is a lockdown.

> TAMARA *groans, stands up.*

This is a lockdown. Sit down, Tamara.

TAMARA: Yeah thanks, Miss. Read my fucking story.

PETCHALL: Language, Tamara. Real or a drill? At that stage I don't know./ He's running straight towards us.

TAMARA/SQUID: He's running straight towards us/ I'm running straight towards her/

SQUID: TO GET THAT FUCKING SLUT.

TO GET THAT FUCKING SLUT!

TO GET THAT FUCKING SLUT!

> *He knocks on the door. Endless knocking. Inside is still. Knocking continues forever.*

I know they're fucking in there, I know they're fucking in there, I know she's fucking in there!

> *Finally...*

TAMARA: Deaf Miss? Can't you hear that?

PETCHALL: It's a lockdown, Tamara. You know the rules.

TAMARA: Fucking stupid, Miss. Someone wants to come in.

PETCHALL: Tamara. Tamara, sit down.

TAMARA: Make me.

> TAMARA, *defiant, opens the door.*

> SQUID *enters with spray paint, stares at* TAMARA, *sprays 'SLUT' on the wall.*

> PETCHALL *tries to stop him, gets in his way but he sprays her dress, her arms. She steps back.*

PETCHALL: Jasyn stop. *Jasyn!*

SQUID: It's English, Miss, and I'm expressing an opinion.

He finishes. Looks at TAMARA.

Why'd you do it?

TAMARA: Not here, Jasyn.

SQUID: Why'd you do it?

PETCHALL: Fans spin slow—spitballs dry on the roof, quiet.

TAMARA: Didn't.

SQUID: You did. You fucked him.

PETCHALL: Sirens wail, pigeon coos on the window sill.

SQUID: You fucking slut, you fucked my brother.

PETCHALL: Kids all around me, kids silent, kids looking at me then at him then at her—then: Everybody out.

Jasyn. Give me the paint. Jasyn.

The rest of you, out! Out now. Go on get out! Kelly put that phone away don't you dare film this get out.

Three of us in the room. Faces at the window.

> PETCHALL *approaches* SQUID. *He pulls out a knife.* PETCHALL *stays between* TAMARA *and* SQUID.

Jasyn, what… what are you doing? Put it down. Put the knife down. Let's calm down here, let's/

SQUID: Tell her what you did?

PETCHALL: Jasyn…

SQUID: Go on. Tell her what you done, Tamara. What you and Dane did the night after he got out of prison? Did you write a story about that too?

> TAMARA *shakes her head.*

Quiet now, are you? First time for everything, isn't there? First time?

> SQUID *and* TAMARA *stare at each other then* SQUID *runs at* TAMARA, *knocks* PETCHALL *over. He holds* TAMARA *with the knife at her neck.*

PETCHALL: Jasyn. Don't. Don't hurt her. You don't want this. Don't… she's… she's just a dumb slut who fucked your brother. You want to fuck up your life? You want to end up like him?

She's just a kid, Jasyn? Jasyn?

SQUID *lets* TAMARA *go. She runs.* PETCHALL *is frozen.* SQUID *collapses onto the floor in tears.*

♦ ♦ ♦

PETCHALL: Every kid in that school that day. Every kid frozen. Still. Frozen in time in silence. And all their faces. Those children's faces. What do I say? To Sol or Phong or Kelly? What do I say?/ I remember Jasyn on his first day of high school.

DANE: I remember Jasyn on his first day of high school.

PETCHALL: New uniform. He came alone. Tried to look like he didn't need anyone there to drop him off, to hold his hand. Came to school and got dropped anyway like a rock to the bottom./ Just like his brother.

DANE: Just like his brother.

♦ ♦ ♦

Several weeks later.

TAMARA: In the days after—Dad said nothing.

Must have known—said nothing.

PETCHALL: On the front page of the paper/ and all over the internet the teen slut stabbing

TAMARA: and all over the internet the teen slut stabbing. Knife didn't go anywhere near me—more hits on YouTube in that first day and/ the way they look at me.

SQUID/PETCHALL: The way they look at me.

PETCHALL: The way girls look at me after what I said about her.

TAMARA: The ladies in the front office the dog-faced news reporter who cut off what I was saying—the leso cop was the only one—she looked at me and smiled said/

TAMARA/PETCHALL: Don't listen to a word anyone says love.

TAMARA/SQUID: Twelve weeks/

TAMARA: Since the Tuesday we started going out. Tuesdays…

SQUID: Aunty shakes her head whispers I'm to blame but never looking at me once not once just whispering/ you're to blame.

TAMARA: I'm to blame/

SQUID: Tellin' me I got one chance or I'm out for good as well—I got one chance at this and if I don't make the best of it then/

TAMARA: It was me. I did this. I did.

TAMARA/SQUID: The police/

SQUID: The court hearing/

TAMARA/SQUID: The counsellor.

TAMARA: Picking her fingernails then turning and asking me…

TAMARA/SQUID: What were you thinking when you did that?

SQUID: Boss at Subway sacks me.

Boss looks at me like I am shit he swept up and kicked in the gutter. Doesn't want the uniform back.

PETCHALL: Parent-teacher night—they sit across the table in the hot hall.

TAMARA/PETCHALL: The look in their eyes/

TAMARA: The counsellor, the girls.

PETCHALL: Parents across a desk whisper thanks but that they're sending their kids somewhere else.

Ask me how on earth can I face it all again after…

Then him: Tamara Brewster's father Laurence at parent-teacher night for the first time ever. Standing in line to speak to me in that hot hall. Sitting down and looking at me like… like/

TAMARA: Mum comes down from Queensland she's turned into a Twistie—orange skin—makes me go to Brisbane—look in her eyes says don't argue and I don't just for once I don't/ fourteen weeks.

SQUID: Fourteen weeks.

TAMARA *leaves.*

Start at the adolescent centre—sign a contract.

Sit in class—reading the same book—*The Outsiders*.

Start boxing.

Speak to this bloke everyday about shit. Tattoos. Dane. 'Feelings'.

SQUID/PETCHALL: Hear shit/ Hear things.

SQUID: Hear they couldn't get the paint off/

PETCHALL: Hear he had taken ice. Ice.

SQUID: Hear she went up north.

PETCHALL: Hear the same song I heard on the earphones that morning— the morning it happened—that song everywhere, in shops, on the radio in the car, in the wind as it whistles through the leaves in the trees.

SQUID: Hear the phone ring. Silent on the other end and I think it's her—
Tamara? I think it's her calling—but it's not.

It's Mum.

She tells me she heard. Says she's gonna try and make it back soon
and when I ask when she goes quiet…

Then.

She's.

Gone.

> SQUID *puts in his iPod and leaves.*

PETCHALL: Girls and boys dressed up for the formal. Eye shadow and
pimples and sweat and milky white tuxedos—taffeta and roses—
heels clattering on concrete. Another year.

> TAMARA *enters in her formal dress and tasselled boots.*

TAMARA: Hello Miss.

PETCHALL: You're back, Tamara.

You look lovely.

TAMARA: Thanks. Can you believe I got this dress in Brisbane?

PETCHALL: And the boots?

TAMARA: And the boots.

TAMARA/PETCHALL: How are you doing?

> *Pause.*

PETCHALL: We should go in.

TAMARA: Yeah.

PETCHALL: Wouldn't want to miss those mocktails.

TAMARA: No.

Miss?

PETCHALL: Yes Tamara?

> *Pause.*

TAMARA: I don't know what to say.

PETCHALL: Then don't say anything, Tamara. Just…

See you in there.

> PETCHALL *goes.* TAMARA *lights a smoke.*

TAMARA: There are formals going on all over Darling Harbour. Limos stopping—bouncers looking tough—hot guys in tuxes, girls giggling—cameras flashing.

The lights from all the places dance on the water—music spills out.

What if they play our song Squid?

You were gonna lift up your shirt on the dance floor—show off your tattoo of the squid god.

Think about texting you but I don't. What would I say?

Think about going in but I don't. Not just yet.

Sixteen weeks ten hours fifteen minutes.

She stubs out her cigarette.

Wonder how I'll remember this.

TAMARA *goes into the formal.*

THE END

GRIFFIN THEATRE COMPANY, AUSTRALIAN THEATRE FOR YOUNG PEOPLE
AND HOTHOUSE THEATRE PRESENT THE WORLD PREMIERE OF

SILENT DISCO
BY LACHLAN PHILPOTT

Silent Disco was co-produced by Griffin Theatre
Company, **atyp** and HotHouse Theatre and had
its world premiere at the SBW Stables Theatre
on 27 April, 2011.

Director Lee Lewis
Designer Justin Nardella
Lighting Designer Ross Graham
Sound Designer/Composer Stefan Gregory
Production Manager Glen Dulihanty

With Camilla Ah Kin, Sophie Hensser,
Kirk Page, Meyne Wyatt

Photography Michael Corridore
Design Interbrand

G T C
R H O
I E M
E A P
E T A
I C R N
I E Y

Last year I saw an exhibition of Tim Burton's drawings and designs in Melbourne. In one display was a book he had written and illustrated as a child, along with the letter of rejection sent to him by the publisher to whom he had submitted the work. In that letter the editor clearly stated that the work was too derivative of Dr. Seuss to be considered original and as such while commendable at his age was not worthy of publication. Early in his creative career the idea of originality was seeded and in his young mind he began to create things he had not seen or heard before.

Truly original voices in the theatre are very rare and I believe that Lachlan Philpott is one of them. He writes like no one else and no one else will write like him. His scripts are authentic, complex, brave, comfortably Australian, and definitely of the 21st century. He is theatrically inventive, formally challenging, linguistically gifted and it is a real privilege to be bringing the first production of his play *Silent Disco* to the Griffin stage. Work like this is what the company was created for and what directors hope to be trusted with. I don't know who it was that seeded in his young head the idea of finding your original voice, but I thank them.

Lee Lewis

DIRECTOR'S NOTE

My Dad Bob was a high school teacher. Kids loved and remembered him long after they left school. Our family could be anywhere and you would hear some voice yelling out 'Bobbie, Bobbie' as some kid, delighted that he existed in the real world too, came up to greet him.

Like many teacher's kids, I ended up as a teacher. *Silent Disco* is a meditation on my time as a secondary school teacher. It aims to celebrate school communities but asks questions about racial and socio-economic disparity in schools.

There are many films and plays written about schools. Some try to impose a hero's journey on the world they represent and in doing so belie mundane rituals and monotonous routines that make most school days endless and forgettable.

Within schools and their strange world of rules, canteen lines, uniforms, colour coded notes, assessments, spit balls and ringing bells, young people learn how to relate to each other. They also forge important relationships with teachers that attempt to empower them as they negotiate the difficult transition to the 'real world'. In this play I focus on these relationships in the context of school community because I am aware that these communities play pivotal roles in connecting people-allowing them to understand each other and in turn themselves.

The play asks what happens when such connections fail?

Many young people seem to aspire to a new kind of materialism and agency. They obsessively 'connect' through technology such as mobile phones, Facebook and iPods. I am interested in exploring how these modes of connection impact on more traditional ones.

I am also interested in telling a teacher's story. Most teachers I know are smart, resilient and dedicated to their work in a way many other professionals find difficult to conceive, particularly in relation to the huge pastoral responsibility they take on every day, every term, every year. In writing this play I wanted to examine that responsibility and how it can affect a teacher on a personal level over a long trajectory.

Since I have left teaching in schools for the moment and chosen to write, I often tussle with the question: How can what I write about be as important as teaching is? It is my hope that this play can matter, like every kid in a school does.

My gratitude to Lee, the cast and creative team, **atyp**, Griffin Theatre Company, HotHouse Theatre and Q Penrith, for supporting the first life to this play.

And thanks to you for coming to experience *Silent Disco*.

Lachlan Philpott

PLAYWRIGHT'S NOTE

Lachlan Philpott
Playwright

For Griffin Theatre Company: Colder.**Other Theatre:** For B Sharp: *Bison*. For atyp: *Bustown*. For wreckedallprods Melbourne: *Catapult*. For NIDA: *Due Monday*. **Other Positions:** Artistic Director Tantrum Theatre 2003-2006, Director of Fresh Ink emerging writers program at The Australian Theatre for Young People between 2008 and 2011. Teaches as part of the post-graduate playwriting and directing courses at NIDA. Awards: Winner Griffin Award for Outstanding New Australian play 2009, Winning Finalist GAP PROJECT Aurora Theatre Co. USA (*Silent Disco*). Winner R.E Ross Trust Award 2007 (*Colder*).**Training:** The VCA (Directing), NIDA (Playwriting).

Lee Lewis
Director

For Griffin Theatre Company: *The Call, The Nightwatchman*. **Other Theatre:** For Sydney Theatre Company: *Honour, ZEBRA!, Love Lies Bleeding*. For Wharf2Loud: *Motel, Stag*. For Belvoir St: *That Face*. For B Sharp: *2000 Feet Away, Half and Half, A Number, 7 Blowjobs*. For Bell Shakespeare: *Twelfth Night*. For Griffin Stablemates: *Stoning Mary*. For Darlinghurst Theatre: *Drowned World, Vicious Streaks*. For Tamarama Rock Surfers: *The Share + The Hour Before My Brother Dies*. For NIDA: *Shopping and F**king, Big Love*. For Theatre Nepean: *Julius Caesar, Trojan Women: A Love Story*. For WAAPA: *As You Like It*. For Short and Sweet: *On That Day*. For New Theatre: *The Tempest, Our Town*. **Other Positions:** As Assistant Director: *Riflemind, The Art of War, Boy Meets Girl* (Sydney Theatre Company). Teaching at NIDA, University of Sydney and NYU. Director of NSW State Schools Senior Drama Ensemble. **Training:** NIDA (Directing), MFA Columbia University (Acting). Currently Associate Director/Literary Advisor, Griffin Theatre Company.

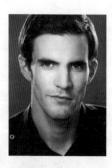

Kai Raisbeck
Assistant Director

For Griffin Theatre Company: Debut. **Other Theatre:** As director: For NIDA: *Vampire Lesbians of Sodom, Electric Eddies World Famous Electricity Show*. For Legs on the Wall: *Tiny Top, Sprout*. For Griffin 24 Hour Play Generator: *Everything is Lovely*. For UTAS: *Play*. As assistant director: For NIDA: *Flight*. For La Mama: *Silence*. **Other Positions:** Affiliate Director, Griffin Theatre Company. **Training:** NIDA

Camilla Ah Kin

Petchall/ Dezzie/ Leanne/ Aunty

For Griffin Theatre Company: *The Nightwatchman, Ship Of Fools*. **Other Theatre:** For Sydney Theatre Company: *Boy Gets Girl, Chasing The Dragon, Playgrounds, Pentecost, The Visit, The Government Inspector*. For Belvoir St Theatre: *Small Poppies, No Sugar*. For Bell Shakespeare: *As You Like It, The Taming Of The Shrew, Macbeth*. For Melbourne Theatre Company: *Like Whiskey On The Breath Of A Drunk You Love, The Flying Doctor, Family Running For Mr. Whippy, The Bear*. For Seymour Centre: *Shafana And Aunt Sarrina*. For Q Theatre: *Milo*. For Ensemble Theatre Company: *Laughter On The 23rd Floor*. For Theatre 20/20: *Three Sisters*. For Chameleon Theatre Company: *The Gap*. For New England Theatre: *Game Of Love And Chance*. For Marian Street: *Sailor Beware!* For WATC: *Our Town, Boss Of The Pool, Dinkum Assorted, The Cherry Orchard*. For Festival of Perth: *Dr. Memory In The Dream Home*. **Film:** *Ali and The Ball, Kangaroo Jack, The Boys, I Eugenia*. **Television:** *All Saints, Stupid Stupid Man, Home And Away, Stories From The Golf, Cnnnn, Backburner, Going Home, Murder Call, Blue Heelers, Halifax F.P.* **Other Positions:** As Director: For Griffin Theatre Company: *Belonging Series*. For ACTT: *Roberto Zucco, Hamlet Discovery Play, Chekhov Projects*. For Monkey Baa Theatre: *Worry Warts*. For Bell Shakespeare: *Who's Laughing Now?* For Theatre 20/20: *The Property Of The Clan*. Dramaturg and Acting tutor for Theatre Nepean (UWS), ACTT, AADA, atyp. **Awards:** 2008 Nomination, Best Supporting Actress, Sydney Theatre Awards *(The Nightwatchman)*. **Training:** University of Sydney, MA (by research), Ecole Internationale du Theatre Jaques Lecoq (Cultural Scholarship). WAAPA.

Sophie Hensser

Tamara

For Griffin Theatre Company: Debut. **Other Theatre:** For Griffin Independent: *The Distance From Here*. For Ensemble Theatre: *It's A Small World, Problem Child*. For Bob Presents: *Summerfolk*. For NIDA: *Cleansed Young Girl*. **Television:** *Cops LAC, Underbelly III, All Saints, Home & Away, The Saddle Club, Bush Patrol*. **Film:** *Bonnie Sweet Robin, The Playground, Driver*. **Awards:** Tim Winton Award for Young Writers, 2005 Page to Stage Winner – Young Dramatists Playwriting Competition. **Training:** NIDA, atyp.

Kirk Page
Dane/ Laurence Brewster /Teacher
For Griffin Theatre Company: Debut. **Other Theatre:** For Sydney Theatre Company: *The Sunshine Club, A Midsummer Night's Dream*. For Belvoir St Theatre: *The Dreamers, Conversations with the Dead*. For Bell Shakespeare: *My Girragundji*. For HotHouse Theatre: *Australia the Show!* For Merrigong Theatre Company: *Death in Bowengabbie*. For Bangarra Dance Theatre: *Ochres*, Closing Olympic ceremony (Atlanta). For Opera Australia: *A Midsummer Night's Dream*. For Legs On The Wall: *Eora Crossing, Runners Up, 4 on the Floor*. For Back Row Productions: *Priscilla*. For Black Swan Theatre Company: *Corrugation Road*. For Malthouse Theatre: *One Night the Moon*. **Film:** *Bloodlines, Shadow Play*. **Other Positions: As Movement Director:** *My Place, Bran Nue Day*. Melbourne Commonwealth Games *My Skin, My Life*.

Meyne Wyatt
Squid
For Griffin Theatre Company: Debut. **Other Theatre:** For Griffin Independent: *The Brothers Size*. For Legs On the Wall/NIDA: *The Hour We Knew Nothing Of Each Other*. For NIDA: *Salome, Accidental Death Of An Anarchist, Lord Of The Flies, Hamlet, Motel, Threepenny Opera Beggar, Gift, Cherry Orchard*. For Aboriginal Theatre/ WAAPA: *Frankenstein And The Lion Of Nemea*. **Training:** NIDA.

Justin Nardella
Designer
For Griffin Theatre Company: Debut. **Other Theatre:** For Sydney Theatre Company: *Before/After*. For B Sharp: *Bliss, Whore, Ladybird*. For Darlinghurst Theatre: *Macbeth, Glace Chase*. For NORPA: *Engine*. For NIDA: *The Shape of Things, Pericles, Love for Love*. **Screen:** *Could be Bad* music video clip for The Scare, *Live and Learn* video clip for Renee Cassar, *Benefit* (short film) **Other positions:** Design Assistant: Global Creatures' Productions *How to Train Your Dragon* and *King Kong*. Events: Brisbane Festival Site designer, Audi, Aveda, UBS, GHD, Audi A8 Launch, Audi Lighthouse Launch, Cointreau Bar and GHD Expert Tour. Part of the Sydney based design studio bright**young**things. **Awards:** The BMW Young Artist Award and The William Fletcher Grant. **Training:** NIDA.

Ross Graham
Lighting Designer
For Griffin Theatre Company: Debut. **Other Theatre:** For B Sharp: *Woyzeck*. For Theatre Row (New York): *Beirut*, *True West*. For Lennox Theatre: *Hat Pin, Yellow Isn't Yellow*. For Perth Playhouse: *Love Bites*. **Other Positions:** Music Credits: *Margot and the Nuclear So and So's*, Melissa Auf De Maur.

Stefan Gregory
Sound Designer and Composer
For Griffin Theatre Company: *The Call*. **Other Theatre:** For Sydney Theatre Company: *The War of the Roses*, *Frankenstein, Baal*. For Belvoir St Theatre: *Wild Duck*, *Measure For Measure, That Face*. For Bell Shakespeare: *King Lear, Hamlet, Othello*. For B Sharp: *A Midsummer Night's Dream, Lady Macbeth of Mtsensk, Ladybird, 2,000 Feet Away*. For the Hayloft Project: *Thyestes, The Suicide, B.C*. **Other Positions:** Associate artist at Belvoir St Theatre in 2011. **Awards:** Platinum Single (*This Heart Attack, Faker*), ARIA nominations for Best Group, Single of the Year & Best Rock Album (*Faker*), Sydney Theatre Awards nomination (*Measure for Measure*), Green Room Award nomination (*Thyestes*).

Production Manager
Glen Dulihanty
For Griffin Theatre Company: *Mister Bailey's Minder National Tour, The Lightkeeper, Woman with Dogs Eyes, The Marvelous Boy, Strangers in Between,* Resident Technical/Production Manager 2004-06. **Other Theatre:** For Belvoir Theatre Company: Full-time Production Deputy 2008-11, Production Manager *Wild Duck, Rubin Guthrie, Man from Mukinupin*. **For International Companies**: For Disney Cruise Lines: Senior Shipwide Technician, For Underbelly @ Edinburgh Festival: Site Manager, *Baby Belly*. For Happy's Circus: Travelling Technician. For The Bush Theatre (London): Full-time Technical Manager. For Theatre4A: Touring Stage Manager *(Hong Kong)*. **Other Positions:** For Playground Weekender, Night Site Manager.

Natasha Marich

Stage Manager

For Griffin Theatre Company: *What's A Girl To Do/ Dorothy Parker Says, Clark In Sarajevo, Speaking In Tongues, Ship of Fools.* **Other Theatre:** For Bell Shakespeare Co: *The Taming of the Shrew.* For Folsom Prison Productions: *The Man in Black - The Johnny Cash Story.* For Critical Stages/Palpable Productions/Darlinghurst Theatre: *The Pitch.* For Red Stitch Actors' Theatre: *The Shape of Things.* For Eddie Perfect/Malthouse Theatre/Sydney Opera House Trust: *Drink Pepsi, Bitch!* For Malthouse Theatre/Sydney Opera House Trust: *The Big Con.* Various productions with visual theatre companies: Keene/Taylor Theatre Project (Melb), Handspan Theatre (Melb), Terrapin Puppet Theatre (Hobart), Company Skylark (ACT); also Playbox Theatre, Melbourne Workers' Theatre, Ilbijerri Aboriginal and Torres Strait Islander Theatre Cooperative, ChamberMade, Melbourne Theatre Company, WomAdelaide, Melbourne International Comedy Festival, Melbourne International Arts Festival. **Other Positions:** Tour/Company Manager for The Flying Fruit Fly Circus' *Circus Girl!,* Regional Arts Victoria; Lighting Designer/ Production Manager for Mainstreet Theatre Company (South Australia) on *The Butcher's Wife* and *The Lightkeeper* , Production Coordinator for the *Sydney Centenary of Federation Celebration* One of the crew with BUSH REPAIR - a company dedicated to the management and restoration of native wildlife habitats & forest reserves in the Limestone Coast region of South Australia. **Training:** Bachelor Of Arts, Visual Arts (Sculpture) - Newcastle College of Advanced Education, NSW; Diploma Of Dramatic Art, Technical Production - NIDA

Griffin Theatre Company

Griffin Theatre Company is Australia's leading new writing theatre and the home of the best Australian stories.

Formed in 1978, Griffin took up residence at the SBW Stables Theatre in 1979. For over 30 years since, the Company has been the boutique powerhouse of Australian theatre: consistently breaking new ground and making an outstanding contribution to the national culture.

Griffin has always been the place to make a great start. Australia's most loved and performed play – Michael Gow's *Away* – premiered at Griffin. The hit films *Lantana* and *The Boys* also began life as plays first produced by the company, as did the TV series *Heartbreak High*. Many artists who now contribute significantly to the Australian theatre, film and television industries began professional careers at Griffin, including Cate Blanchett, Jacqueline McKenzie and David Wenham.

In recent years, this success has continued with smash hits like *Angela's Kitchen* and *Speaking In Tongues*, and return seasons and national and international tours of plays including *Savage River, The Story of the Miracles at Cookie's Table, Mr Bailey's Minder* and *Holding the Man*.

Now, Griffin is the only professional theatre company in Sydney entirely dedicated to the development and production of new Australian plays. Presenting four or five productions each year, Griffin regularly tours across Australia. The company also acts as a hub for artists and audiences alike; co-presenting the best independent theatre in Sydney through Griffin Independent; providing audiences with diverse and innovative experiences through Griffringe and Griffin *Between the Lines;* nurturing the theatre-makers of tomorrow through our education program, the Griffin Ambassadors; and harnessing the talents of the country's best emerging writers and directors through our groundbreaking resident artist scheme, the Griffin Studio.

Griffin aims to develop and stage the best new Australian stories, in the most exciting theatre in the country, for the widest possible audience.

Griffin Theatre Company

13 Craigend St, Kings Cross NSW 2011
Phone: 02 9332 1052
Fax: 02 9331 1524
Email: info@griffintheatre.com.au
Web: griffintheatre.com.au

SBW Stables Theatre

10 Nimrod St
Kings Cross NSW 2011
Online bookings at griffintheatre.com.au
or call 02 8019 0292

ABOUT GRIFFIN

In 2010, we teamed up with our pals at Tonkin Zulaikha Greer to give the SBW Stables a well-earned renovation. It's time to give playwrights a better home, and we've already started down the road to making the old Stables more comfortable and safer for artists and audiences alike.

Tonkin Zulaikha Greer, while also being the perfect firm for the job with their experience working on a multitude of historically and culturally significant sites, have been integral to the project for their vision and the generosity as sponsors of the project.

But TZG weren't the only ones; we've had a groundswell of support for the project from theatre fans all around the country, and we're so grateful!

But there is still more to do... stage two will encompass a refit of the theatre itself – stay tuned for more information – but rest assured it will include a more ergonomic seating solution for our audiences and an improved operator space for our hardworking stage managers.

If you think the refit of the SBW Stables Theatre is pretty darn exciting and something you'd like to be part of, you should give our Development Manager, Allie Townsend, a call on 9332 1052 or drop her a line on philanthropy@griffintheatre.com.au. Donors at brick level and above will be acknowledged in perpetuity in the foyer.

CAPITAL
WORKS
PROGRAM

Beam ($120,000+)
Seaborn, Broughton & Walford Foundation

Pillar ($45,000)
Bluptons
Tonkin Zulaikha Greer
Ros Horin & Joe Skrzynski
Rockend Technology Pty Ltd
ArtsNSW
Rebel Penfold-Russell
Kim Williams

Step ($15,000)
Antoinette Albert
Charmaine & Michael Bradley
Lewin Family
Nick Marchand & Nathan Bennett
Ezekiel Solomon
Stuart Thomas
Townsend Family

Brick ($3,000)
Gillian Appleton
Baker & McKenzie
Baly Douglass Foundation
John Bell & Anna Volska
Gina Bowman, Sally Noonan & Mark Sutcliffe
BOSE
Jo Briscoe & Brenna Hobson
Rob Brookman & Verity Laughton
Bob & Helena Carr
Ange Cecco & Melanie Bienemann
Rae & Russ Cottle
Glyn Cryer
Alison Deans & Kevin Powell
David Farley
Nicki Bloom & Geordie Brookman
Richard Glover
Peter Graves, Canberra
Maurice Green AM & Christina Green
The Griffins – Allie, Bel, Jas & Jen
Larry & Tina Grumley
Mary & John Holt
Ken & Lilian Horler
The Actors' Centre
Chris Jackman
Currency Press
Peter, Angela & Piper Keel
Brett Boardman & Lee Lewis
Lisa Mann Creative Management'
Wendy McCarthy AO
Sophie McCarthy & Tony Green
Bruce Meagher & Greg Waters
Dianne O'Connell
Peter O'Connell
Debra Oswald
Ian Phipps
Peace of Mind Technology
Celina Pront
Joel Pront
Chris Puplick AM
Chris & Fran Roberts
Ian Robertson
Mike Robinson
Signwave Newtown
Cre8ion
Will Sheehan
Kate & David Sheppard
Diana Simmonds
Smith & Jones
Chris Tooher & Rebecca Tinning

Current as at 4.3.11

Patron Seaborn, Broughton and Walford Foundation
Board Michael Bradley (Chair), Hilary Bell, Damian Borchok, Lisa Lewin (Treasurer), Sophie McCarthy, Leigh O'Neill, Kate Sheppard, Sam Strong and Stuart Thomas

Artistic Director Sam Strong
General Manager Simon Wellington
Finance Manager Alison Baly
Production Manager Micah Johnson
Artistic Associate Belinda Kelly
Marketing Manager Jennifer Cannock
Development Manager Allie Townsend
Administration Coordinator Lizzie Cater
Front-of-House Manager Jasmine De Carlo
Front-of-House Supervisor Paige Rattray
Associate Director/Literary Advisor Lee Lewis
Affiliate Directors James Dalton and Kai Raisbeck
Griffin Studio Ian Meadows, Kate Mulvaney, Shannon Murphy, Paige Rattray

Writers under commission
A Playwriting Australia Co-Commission
Jane Bodie *(This Year's Ashes)*

Web Developer House of Laudanum
Brand and Graphic Design Interbrand
Photography Michael Corridore
Printing Whirlwind

Griffin donors
Income from Griffin activities covers less than 50% of our operating costs – leaving an ever increasing gap for us to fill through government funding, sponsorship and the generosity of our individual supporters. Your support helps us bridge the gap and keep ticket prices affordable and our work at its best. To make a donation and a difference, contact Griffin on 9332 1052 or donate online at griffintheatre.com.au.

Production ($10,000+)
Anonymous (2)
James & Jeanne-Claude Strong

Rehearsal ($5,000–$9,999)
Ezekiel Solomon
Tony Green
Sophie McCarthy

Griffin Studio ($5,000)
Gil Appleton
Tony Green
Sophie McCarthy

Workshop ($1,000–$4,999)
Anonymous (1)
Actors Centre Australia
Gil Appleton
Baly Douglass Foundation
David & Anne Bennett
Charmaine & Michael Bradley
Richard Cottrell
Larry & Tina Grumley
Stephen Manning
Geoff & Wendy Simpson
Augusta Supple

Reading ($500–$999)
Jennifer Ledgar & Bob Lim
Ros & Paul Espie
Gadens Lawyers
Michelle Gortan
John & Mary Holt
Ken & Lillian Horler
Peter & Angela Keel
Leigh O'Neill
Anthony Paull
Robin Rodgers
Michelle Shek & Harry Brilliant
Isla Tooth
Louise Walsh & Dave Jordan
Peter Wojtowizc

First Draft ($200–$499)
Jes Andersen
Jason Bourne
Katharine Brisbane
Julia & Nick Brooke
Wendy Buswell
Peter Chapman
Telina Clarke
Vic Cohen & Rosie McColl
Mullinars Casting Consultants
Elizabeth Evatt
Peter Graves
Jennifer Hagan
Janet Heffernan
Margaret Johnston
Henry Johnston
Lou Lander
Jean Prouvaire
Nick Marchand
Christopher McCabe
Neville Mitchell
Rod Phillips
Roslyn Renwick
Catherine Rothery
Roz Tarszisz
Douglas Trengove
Bill Winspear

Current as at 04.03.11

GRIFFIN STAFF & DONORS

Griffin would like to thank the following

Patron

Griffin acknowledges the generosity of the Seaborn, Broughton and Walford Foundation in allowing it, since 1986, the use of the SBW Stables Theatre rent free, less outgoings.

2011 Season Sponsors

Production Sponsor

Monday Rush Sponsor

Associate Sponsors

Company Sponsors

Foundations and Trusts

Government Sponsors

Griffin Theatre Company is assisted by the Australian Government through the Australia Council, its arts funding and advisory body and the NSW Government through Arts NSW.

GRIFFIN
SPONSORS